I

QUIT

PLASTICS

and you can too

This book belongs to _____ .

With the intention: _____

We create this humble guide in the spirit of sharing ideas, spreading solutions and empowering change-makers to be bold and courageous.

With deep reverence, we honour all resources consumed for these pages.

Setting the intention that our positive impact will ripple outward, inspiring others.

Honouring these pages that once were trees reaching for the sun.

The water used to make the paper.

Blessing any chemicals that flowed from this process, may this book outdo any harm caused.

We honour the humans whose hands bound this book and packed the boxes.

We honour the dinosaur bones that burned as fuel to transport this book.

We will absorb and learn and grow and shift to make all of the effort and output worthwhile.

We value this book. We value our things. We vote with our dollar.

We are mindful of our choices. We are conscious of our impact.

We do our best. We come from love.

We are not saving nature, we are nature.

I QUIT PLASTICS

60+ lifestyle recipes to cut waste,
live clean and change the world

KATE NELSON

LOST
THE
PLOT

LOST
THE
PLOT

A Lost the Plot book, first published in 2020 by Pantera Press Pty Limited
www.PanteraPress.com

Please send all permission queries to:
Pantera Press, P.O. Box 1989, Neutral Bay, NSW, Australia 2089 or info@PanteraPress.com

A Cataloguing-in-Publication entry for this book is available from the National Library of Australia.
ISBN 978-1-925700-60-2 (Paperback)

Cover and internal design: Elysia Clapin
Publisher: Martin Green
Editor: Anne Reilly
Proofreaders: Anna Blackie and Lucy Bell
Printed and bound by Asia Pacific Offset China

Dedicated to the PlasticFreeMermaid community.

Thank you for supporting me always.

Thank you for your efforts and contribution.

We are in this together. And many of you have been with me since before

sustainability was cool or world-saving was urgent.

I'm so grateful to have the opportunity and platform

to share what I have learned along the way.

Thank you for being with me.

Dedicated to the wildlife — including us rewilding sapiens — that we all

may ingest less plastic because of this book.

Contents

Author's note

Thank you for picking up this book. I hope you find *I Quit Plastics* a resource and a gateway to reconnect with our wondrous planet, Earth. Quitting single-use plastics is not the only path we can take. In fact, every choice we make with positive environmental outcomes is a drop that, when multiplied by millions of people, becomes a mighty river. It is through these individual changes that we can collectively draw civilisation back into harmony with nature.

This book supports us to make small changes to move away from disposable packaging, away from processed food, away from our throwaway culture and conditioning for overconsumption. It supports us to honour our reliance on a healthy, thriving planet. Empowers us to acknowledge that we breathe air into our lungs, eat vegetation that sprouts from dirt, drink water that falls from the sky. We are a part of these ecosystems and our actions either support or harm the soil. This guide encourages us to cultivate our relationship with nature, so we see that when we pollute the air, we pollute ourselves. When we carelessly waste plastic, we hurt our children. When we deplete the soil, we deplete our food, which depletes our bodies. We are not separate from the environment. We *are* nature.

Many of us are waking up and remembering this. Instead of pointing the finger at those who do not acknowledge our inextricable integration with nature, let's focus on being the most shining examples and channel our energy towards creating the harmonious world we dream of. I hope that this book will inspire changes in purchasing habits and openings in mindfulness. Giving up disposable plastics causes us to rethink our shopping lists, break free from routines that may or may not be serving us and become more aware of who we support with our dollars. Once we learn how detrimental plastic is, our attention is on high alert to avoid the material. Something opens in our minds and we are able to see plastics that have been there all along.

All of this ethical strategising cultivates increased presence in other aspects of life, as well as feelings of fulfilment, purpose and happiness. It connects us back to what we spend our money on. What we spend our energy on. Helps us re-evaluate how we use our time, what we value, who we choose to connect with, and how we want to feel. Quitting plastics is an invitation to mindfulness. It is a coming back to who we have always been.

This is a humbling journey. I grew up eating packaged, processed foods. I wasted hundreds of plastic cups at college parties. I bought disposable plastics and didn't think twice about throwing them 'away'. When I had my plastics awakening, I was incredibly disturbed at my own oblivious contribution to the mounting pollution. And I was empowered to honour my agency as a human being. I refused to stay, unquestioning, in the fast-moving flow of mass consumption causing mass pollution. I chose to step into my sovereignty and make my own choices. I would celebrate being different. I wouldn't push; I would lead by example and inspire others to join me. I would choose flowers and herbs and water and sky and grass and oils and vegetables.

There are many ways to live more ecologically in sync. One way is to choose the materials you touch. Quitting plastics enabled me to touch more plants, wood, glass, metal. A foreshadowing aesthetic preference that kept me out of shopping malls and supacentres, leading me instead to shop and harvest in gardens. Not having plastic-free make-up options moved me to eat healthier, get lots of sleep and exercise, so that I didn't rely on make-up to feel beautiful or comfortable in my skin. With plastic-packaged crackers and dips off limits, I made my own. Never truly domestically inclined, I laughed through my efforts to sew ripped clothing and bake my own breads. For the ocean — my playground, my temple and the essence of this water planet which all life depends on — learning to make my own hummus was no burden or sacrifice. It was an honour. Even if the first few batches were far from delicious!

Our minds are elastic and we can alter our patterns, master our habits and reframe our experiences. I witnessed plastic evolve from a packaging material into a socially destructive mechanism for separation and division. Its presence indicated 'this has been tampered with', so I established new habits and neurological pathways to abstain from plastic. Through this daily ethical challenge, I learned deeply what it felt like to live the vibration of integrity. I understood how to support the economy of products that align with my values. Through my choices and purchases, I could slowly construct the world I dreamed of.

A decade ago, my choice to quit using plastics was extreme. It led me on an adventure full of wild characters, peppered with hilarity, confusion, courage and humility. I am incredibly grateful for the lifestyle that grew from this potent seed. I wish you a light, joyous approach as you experiment with how you truly want your one precious life to look and feel. This is a chance to rewrite your story, to compost what is no longer serving you in your life and create the world you dream of living and thriving in.

Thank you for reading this. I am beyond grateful. It was a great joy to write these words. I rewrote them often, as I am learning every day on this incredible adventure. It was hard to turn in a 'complete' version because our planet is changing so much every day and the social climate is evolving so quickly. It has been humbling to step away and let these words stand on their own.

Having finished work on this book, I return to my passion of environmental activism, so this is what your purchase supports.

Thank you.

Sincerely,
Kate

1

THE PATH

'Don't be too timid and squeamish about your actions. All life is an experiment. The more experiments you make the better.'

— RALPH WALDO EMERSON

My start

In 2008, I was volunteering for Dr Andrea Neal in Santa Barbara, California, at Jean-Michel Cousteau's Ocean Futures Society. There I learned that plastic does not biodegrade and that it was collecting in large whirpool-like systems called 'gyres' in between continents. Shocked and horrified, I tracked down Captain Charles Moore, who discovered the Great Pacific Trash Gyre, to learn more. And soon I was aboard a University of Hawaii research vessel, venturing out there to witness for myself the destruction. What I discovered was that the ocean in this gyre was a beautiful blue soup, thick with plastic bits.

Facing the severity and scale of this issue, I took a drastic step and quit single-use plastics. I became an advocate and lobbied the government, pitched to corporates, spoke at schools all over the world, met with any politician who would hear me and co-founded an education and advocacy non-profit called 'Save the Mermaids' that is still going strong today, thanks to the dedication and passion of my mermaid sisters.

I learned how to use social media as a tool to communicate information about plastic pollution and my lifestyle. Depressing statistics were balanced with inspiring tips, easy recipes, tales from my adventures to reawaken the wonder and a healthy dash of mermaid cheekiness to keep these changes feeling positive and appealing. I moved to Australia, where my love for dancing on waves and diving in the sea was nourished by the incredibly vibrant marine environment and I felt aligned with the community's budding affinity for earth-centric living.

I've expanded beyond just single-use plastics and avoid as much plastic as possible in my life. Any waste that I am responsible for that is not recyclable and which would end up in landfill, I keep. I store it in a large mason jar and at the end of the year I can take a look at all of the trash I couldn't avoid!

So, here I am — still a cheeky mermaid sharing her tips and recipes with as many folks who will listen. I teach my ways through various digital platforms such as iquitplastics.com and @plasticfreemermaid. I host magical mermaid retreats where I bring people on epic ocean adventures to reconnect with the wonder of nature — swimming with whales, sailing around tropical islands, freediving with dolphins. I also teach yoga, my plastic-free ways, strategies for environmental activism and how to step into power and purpose. (I cancelled all mermaid retreats for 2019 to eliminate the carbon burned to transport us to the magical destinations.) Grateful for the opportunity and so encouraged by the growing interest, I stay grounded by practising yoga, getting in the ocean, drinking lots of water, and eating as healthily as my sweet tooth allows. I practise patience, gratitude and surrendering to the humble balance between ocean and digital communications technology.

Why quit plastics?

OUR EARTH, OUR LIFE

We rely on food growing from the ground, we breathe air, we drink water. We need this planet to remain in good health for our own survival. According to 'The New Plastics Economy' (2016) published by the World Economic Forum, the plastics industry has been ramping up production over recent decades — growing from 15 million tonnes annually in 1964 to 311 million tonnes in 2014, with growth projected to continue. By weight there will be more plastic than fish in the sea by 2050. Currently, the equivalent of one garbage truck of trash gets dumped into the oceans every minute of every day.

Plastic pollution is out of control and not slowing down. The cause of this pollution is our consumption of products manufactured by big corporations. We could focus on the clean-up of pollution, which is important, but given the constant addition of more pollution, isn't entirely effective. If the sink was overflowing, you wouldn't start mopping the floor, you'd turn off the tap. Same principle. We need to address the source of the plastics flooding into our environment. We can focus on reducing our own consumption of plastics. By refusing to buy plastic-packaged goods, we lower the demand for them. Additionally, we can be vocal about our preferences for more 'regenerative' packaging and products. Do this by writing to store managers and business owners and sharing to your networks that you refuse to buy from businesses that don't honour the environment, and will shop elsewhere or go without unless they reduce the amount of plastics they're producing. To get involved in large-scale activism, I recommend you look into the #BreakFreeFromPlastic movement.

SHORT-TERM HEALTH

Food is the fuel the body runs on. If a food product is packaged in sealed plastic, it's often also processed and full of ingredients that are technically edible, but neither natural to our digestive tract nor easy to obtain nutrition from. It's challenging trying to discern nutritional value from long lists of unrecognisable ingredients and preservatives. When we fill up on vibrant fruits, vegetables, legumes and whole grains instead, we avoid this headache of assessing health values. The positive impacts of making salads and fresh stir-fries are felt from the empty trash bin, to the growing compost bin, to the happy body!

LONG-TERM HEALTH

Plastic leaches toxic chemicals. This means that plastic packaging can contaminate whatever it contains — food, drink, cosmetics, etc. Toxins leach in three instances: when the contents are hot, contain fat, or are stored for a long period of time. Let this sink in. These are pretty common conditions.

Toxins leach when plastic gets hot. This happens anytime we microwave food in plastic, have drink bottles or containers in a hot climate, or place any hot substance in Tupperware. Realising that takeaway food comes only in plastic, I started bringing a large glass jar when I went to get takeout. Since this cuisine is generally hot and greasy, the plastic from the takeaway boxes would leach into the food! Second, the chemicals in plastics are lipophilic, or attracted to fat. So the greasy takeaway is a target for toxins because of the high oil content. If you have a latte, the plastic chemicals are attracted to the fat in the milk. Things like body butters or oils stored in plastic are likely to contain leached chemicals.

Look around your house and notice any plastic containers that you've had for a long while, like shelf-stable milks or plastic-wrapped snack bars. Even if they are labelled organic or natural, they have not accounted for the harmful contamination from the packaging.

Why are the leached chemicals so unhealthy? They mimic oestrogen in the body. The gradual build-up of these leached chemicals inside us is contributing to a range of health issues, including higher incidences of weight gain, depression and infertility. And this doesn't stop with just us: the impacts on our reproductive systems may be passed on to our offspring for generations to come.

Biochemist Dr Anthony Jay opened my eyes to this big reason we need to quit plastics. If you'd like to know more, see www.ajconsultingcompany. com for links to his podcasts and book, *Estrogeneration* (Pyrimidine Publishing). Dr Leo Trasande further expanded on the seriousness of the hormone-disrupting toxins as well as the economic implications on nations populated by citizens with declining health and IQ in his book, *Fatter, Sicker, Poorer* (Houghton Mifflin Harcourt Publishing Co.).

ENVIRONMENTAL IDENTIFICATION

Just like participating in recycling, giving up some plastics helps people to identify more as environmentalists. This spills into other aspects of life causing them to behave more earth-centrically – they may engage in a climate emergency debate, support a political candidate who pledges to protect the environment or only spend their money on sustainable businesses.

QUALITY OF LIFE

We feel better about ourselves for making better choices for the planet and future generations. With healthier choices, our well-being improves. We're making more things at home, perhaps slowing down a bit. We may get to know local producers and like-minded people in our community. In short, we feel more in tune with nature and better able to live a more connected, enriched life.

FUTURE GENERATIONS

From our children to endangered species, the negative consequences of plastics overuse reach far beyond the waste generated by single-use plastics. It's irresponsible to opt for a moment's convenience without thinking of the long-term effect of our choices. Extinction is forever and the natural habitat is stressed enough from the climate crisis. Just because a packaged product is available and cheap, it doesn't mean we're entitled to buy it. With a little inventiveness, we can collectively shift demand to create a plastic-free marketplace. We can do it. We *have* to.

Already the pollution we're living with is too much.

NOW OR NEVER

It's time for all of us individuals to create a better world as of right now. Start with your plastics, your footprint, your personal impact. Then you can feel good about demanding better solutions of our leaders.

The present moment is all we have. 'Later' is too late. 'Someday' may never come. This book is an invitation to take it slow and start small and commit to phasing out single-use plastics. There are exciting new trends around environmentalism. Jump on it! Don't wait to take action to benefit our planet.

This versus that

Here are a few everyday scenarios showing life with plastics versus life without, just to help put this all into perspective.

OPTION A   Go to the big supermarket and buy the plastic-packaged basil.

PROS

I have to go to this store because I need to buy toilet paper, shampoo, washing powder, clothes pegs, notebooks, apples, sparkling water and avocados anyway, so I'll just add it to the list. It costs me $3 for a bunch. I can take the basil home and put it in a glass of water and it will last four or five more days. If it starts to wilt, I can blend it into pesto and freeze it or preserve it with lemon and oil. (Must factor in the time it takes to make and clean up for this task.)

CONS

It's packaged in plastic, which will take around 1000 years to break down and is likely to end up in the oceans in the meantime, wreaking havoc on our already highly stressed marine ecosystems and entering the food chain to amplify the negative impact. The basil could get crushed by all the heavier shopping items on the way home. If it wilts before use, this creates food waste, which emits methane into the atmosphere. The negatives stack up if the herb does wilt: it never serves its purpose of enhancing our meals, so we lose $3; we also create greenhouse gases; plus we let plastic loose into the world for the next ten centuries. And how will I ever use an entire bunch of basil in four days? I barely have time to blend up pesto!

OPTION B   Buy a small basil plant for $5 or a seed pack for half the price. Take 10 minutes to go to the backyard and dig up some dirt, put it into a pot, a wide-mouthed jar or a deep bowl and put the plant in. Water, keep on the windowsill in sunshine, use the leaves as needed and snip off the top if it goes to seed.

PROS

I planted a thing! I'm contributing to the circle of life. I feel connected to nature. I'm also helping to reduce carbon in our atmosphere because plants drink in CO_2. I got my hands dirty, and touching dirt is an important grounding practice: it keeps us from looking too far forward, too far out to space; it maintains some awareness of the earth as the ground where all of our food grows — whether we grew it or not. I feel accomplished and satisfied by caring for a plant. I'm inspired, and maybe this will lead to planting other herbs and produce. I can pick only what I need instead of having to use an entire bunch over the course of four days. I have fresh herbs for weeks to come, as my plant will survive for as long as I remember to water it and monitor its exposure to sunshine.

CONS

The 10 minutes I spend planting a little bush could have been spent scrolling on Instagram. Have to go outside into the hot sun; my fingernails fill up with dirt. Have to remember to water the plant. Maybe it will die! Then $5 will be lost and the dead plant will have to go into compost.

SITUATION 2 *I desire to pamper myself with beauty products.*

OPTION A   I go to the beauty shop, walk the many aisles stacked full of products and select a few tubes and containers that promise tighter and more glowing skin.

PROS

Depending on the store, it might have cost you as little as $20, so nice one on the bargain. You go home and spread the stuff on and instantly feel a tightening and see a nice glow on the skin. You can then arrange your goodies on the shelf and use them whenever you feel the need for a little pick-me-up.

CONS

You drove to the store just for some beauty products. Depending on the store, it may have cost you $100 to $200; there are other things you could have done with this money, including donating to a political campaign fighting for climate justice. Also, there's absolutely no doubt that the packaging for these products uses some plastic, which lasts on the planet for ten times this lifetime. Not to mention the products likely contain chemicals that might help you to look nice at the first application, but over time could be harmful as they build up in your body. This is especially true of chemicals that leach from the plastic container into the product and then into your body. While spreading this cream and gel all over you will make you feel and look better, would you eat the stuff, with all those synthetic chemicals? If not, then you probably shouldn't put it on your skin, because it will be absorbed into your body. And will you really use all of this product within its expiry date? If so, $100 well spent. If not, what a waste. Then, afterwards, you have to dispose of the container. Where does it go? There's a high chance of it washing up on a beach somewhere in 20 years.

OPTION B   Invest in a bottle or two of organic oil. Try starting with coconut oil and grape seed oil (preferably in glass with a metal lid). Gather a few flowers or herbs. You can pick fresh or buy dried from a shop selling loose tea. Wash face with the oils, then splash cool tea on face as a toner (green tea to tighten, chamomile to soothe). Or spread fresh aloe vera gel across the face to tighten the skin. To moisturise, dab skin with flower- or herb-infused oil.

PROS

It costs between $10 and $30 for a few jars of oil and some tea. The oil will never go bad as long as you keep water out of it. The tea is dry and can be used for toning anytime. Don't forget the benefit of multi-use: you can also drink the tea! If you ever have a surprise guest, you have another choice of tea on hand for a little hospitality. In terms of efficiency, it takes the same amount of time to apply oil to your face as it does to apply a store-bought cream. The oil is natural, organic even, and because it's sold as a food product, you know it's safe to put on your skin. Natural oil is moisturising if applied with water, which is why you wash with it first and then tone with tea. The tea is hydrating and, depending on the herbs you use, also provides different effects to balance the skin. As for aloe vera gel, we know it's a phenomenal burn healer, which tells us it has incredible affinity with skin.

Perfect! Use it daily to heal scars and any blemishes. It can be grown indoors or outdoors and requires basically zero love to flourish, so hopefully you have access to a plant either at your own home or else you can locate one nearby at a neighbour's. All this touching of plants and making of teas is healthy. It reconnects us with earthly things. We eat plants, we drink water, we need sunshine — we are earthly and thrive when in harmony with nature. When we pamper ourselves with oils and plants, we can look after ourselves without subjecting our bodies to chemicals with unknown lasting consequences.

CONS

It's easy to place our trust in a product claiming to tighten the skin. It's easy to simply pay for that product — even if the physical result doesn't happen it could have psychological benefits. The chemicals in the packaged product might really work, and without any lasting damage done to the body; who knows! Having to make a tea for a facial toner requires walking to the kitchen and turning on the kettle — the urge for glowing skin may pass by the time the water boils. Pouring oil out of a bottle into the palm of your hand is less convenient than squeezing a small, containable dollop of cream from a tube. If I rinse my face with water after washing with oil, over time the oil could build up in the sink pipes and cause blockages.

Before you take that first step

REGENERATIVE > SUSTAINABLE

It's promising that our collective connection with nature is becoming more refined, meaning that we must constantly evolve our vocabulary as well in order to articulate the relationship. 'To sustain' is to maintain where we are for a long period of time. This sounded good until we realised that what we have now isn't sustainable, so we need to back up and recreate the systems that are broken to make them worth sustaining to begin with.

The word 'regenerate' makes more sense. Let's regenerate the systems, the politics, the soil. Turn the dirt, compost the scraps, and create rich soil in which to plant crops. The more we work in harmony with nature to guide and shape our systems, the more grounded the systems will be. Sturdy, stable, supportive and ecological — taking all beings' well-being into account.

FIRST THINGS FIRST

If you make the choice to quit plastics, it is a comprehensive mental shift to approach all purchases, meals and product interactions differently. We're actively digging up the mental programming we've been raised with — including the societal conditioning to be good consumers. We're raking and hoeing this mental soil, preparing it for values such as minimalism and self-sufficiency to take root. As these concepts begin to feel like your own, you'll find in this book plenty of tips for sustaining these choices and maintaining this rich, tended soil to support the budding mind-forest of a fulfilling, abundant, luxurious plastic-free life.

How to quit plastics

SET A TARGET

This will vary depending on the time, energy, resources and climate you have to work with. Start with eliminating one to five plastic habits within a specific timeframe.

When I first quit single-use plastics, I considered this to include cups, bottles, bags and straws. This helped me focus on developing specific new habits, such as bringing my own bottle and refilling often, making it clear I didn't want a straw before the drinks arrived, getting creative if I forgot my shopping bag and using a box, or bringing multiple cups for myself and my friends to events.

WASTE AUDIT

If you feel like you are pretty sorted with your reusable cup habits and you're ready to make more comprehensive changes, you are ready to conduct a Waste Audit. Collect all of your trash for one or two weeks. Try to choose a week you do your shopping and have a pretty normal routine. Keep everything. All the sauce packets, zip-ties, elastic bands, bits of plastic film, lids, mail, etc. At the end of the week, dump the bin out onto a tarp and sort through all of the waste to create a list of where your waste comes from. Write down yoghurt tub, carton (tetra pak), soft drink bottle, produce bag, etc.

We are turning off the tap of plastics by identifying the source of the waste. Once we have this list, we can go along and identify alternatives for each item.

MAKE A PLAN

Once the alternatives to the plastics you currently use are decided upon, then it is time to plan the action items, such as shopping, making or planting. If, for example, you decide to try making coconut yoghurt instead of buying plastic packaged, you would want to carve out sufficient time in your week to fit in this task. If you decide to make porridge or chia pudding, allow yourself time to get to the health shop or bulk food store to collect the necessary ingredients. Try to stay as organised as possible when you are first trying to quit these pesky plastics. They are literally designed for our convenience, so if you get all the way home from the bulk store to realise you forgot something, this could cause a negative association with this process and we want to avoid this at all costs!

Many of our plastic woes stem from food packaging. To ensure the plastic-packaged chips or frozen dinners don't get tossed in the cart in a fit of frustration, weakness or exhaustion:

* Pre-plan meals.
* Create a shopping list, specifying the locations where the items will be purchased.
* Create a list of things to make (a making list), prioritising essential items you will use daily over the treat items.
* Set the shopping plan based on opening hours, locations and your work/commitment schedule; organise your week to fit in the farmers' market, bulk store, etc.
* Carve out a few hours for making. This may be time to prep the meals, make a large batch of bean dip or plant milk or set up the products you need for general cleaning.
* Make time for nature.

Above all, just keep trying. And don't beat yourself up if you fall off the horse; this is about the long game. Get back on and start again!

KEEP TRACK OF THE CHANGES

As you shift away from plastics, it may be worth keeping a journal to record and clarify your thoughts around what you're experiencing. You're changing your food products, you're changing your cleaning products, you're changing your bath products. You're shopping less and making more of what you consume. You're spending more time outside in the garden and at farmers' markets, and less time inside crowded superstores. You're also connecting more with other humans. Be aware and witness yourself as you make all of these changes to your lifestyle. Where are you feeling more connected? Are there areas where you feel more stressed? How does it feel for your body? Mind? Spirit? Heart?

Notice if we find ourselves viewing this as a forced quitting of a comfortable lifestyle. We can reframe this experience as a gentle courtship with nature, a remembering of how we used to live, a reintegration of what we feel deeply and know well. We can take the pressure off. This is an act of remembering. Our people have gone quite far away from nature. Into buildings with processed air, hard floors that block out the earth, ceilings that block out the sky. Savour the experience of connecting back to Earth. She needs us just as we need her. Observe and be patient as this relationship and harmony re-establish. Enjoy the process.

CHEAT DAY

You can always have some lenience. If you struggle. If you miss your crackers or tempeh. If you love a particular shampoo or nothing cleans like a certain product that only comes in a plastic bottle, maybe a cheat day is the solution. Perhaps, as you wean yourself off all the other plastics in your life, you can make a few allowances in order to stay sane.

As you start out, you may want to try one cheat day a month. It can help you to rein in your overall plastic purchases if you have one day a month to shop the naughty list. Ideally, we slowly find alternatives and the cheat-day list is reduced so that eventually the frequency of cheat days goes down as well.

There are always options. If you're buying food for your family or household, you may need a plastics cheat day once a week!

PLASTIC SWEAR JAR

The swear jar is a gentle way of helping with a swearing habit. Each time someone in the household swears, they have to put a dollar in the jar. The plastics swear jar accumulates wealth if a housemate or family member brings plastic in or buys plastic on a non-cheat day! Agree ahead of time where the money will be donated at the end of the year; do what's possible within your means. Be patient and compassionate with yourself. We can only do our best!

TRASH JAR

While I'm talking about jars, might as well tell you about where I keep my trash. Instead of putting non-recyclable plastics and clothing and other trash into the landfill bin to put it into someone else's care, *I keep it.* I put it in a jar that I've named my #trashjar. I am forever a student and forever wanting to learn and be better, so I check it and figure out how I can get leaner in my wastage.

And I am not perfect! What goes into the trash jar? Plastic luggage tags, fruit stickers, plastic clothing tags from op shops, coconut oil jar freshness seals, the occasional surfing casualty like a leash, plastic festival wristbands, etc.

TIPS TO MAKE QUITTING PLASTICS SUSTAINABLE

* Do your best.
* Be strict with yourself but don't be too hard on yourself.
* Enjoy the shifts, the lessons and the learnings.
* Don't just quit buying plastics. Embrace your *sovereignty as a consumer*.
* View these choices, acts, changes as part of your self-love practice.
* Reframe 'going without' or 'giving something up' as an investment in your health, well-being and an enriched lifestyle.
* Each act returns you to nature – how romantic is this intentional reawakening!

How to keep going

Quitting plastics is a journey. Words of inspiration have helped to keep me going at every stage, and I hope words will help keep you going too. I've returned time and again to the following philosophies. They've been lights to navigate by, and I've repeated them to myself hundreds of times.

WE'RE ONLY RESPONSIBLE FOR OURSELVES

You are a sovereign being. You are responsible only for what you do. You are not responsible for others. You can be in charge of your own impact on the world. Tackling the waste you create matters and is manageable. It won't happen overnight, so bring patience and compassion for yourself.

Practise compassion for those around you who have not vowed to quit plastics; they may not be ready to take this on yet. You're not responsible for them. This can be super hard to accept once you're filled with the passion for a cleaner planet and the urgency with which we need change. I totally get it. I've been there.

It can feel almost like a personal attack when someone we love or live with refuses to wipe out all of the plastics in their life too. Take deep breaths and remember that we're all on our own journey and others may need more time to let go. Don't nit-pick and debate. Explain your reasoning and share what you know but be sensitive and do not aggravate your relationships over this. The best way to handle these situations is simply to show a beautiful example of this lifestyle. They will eventually come around. But if they don't, then your values may be misaligned. I would advise against pointing fingers at anyone else (mega corporations doing the wrong thing or complete sell-out politicians excepted). Definitely not until you have few, if any, changes to make to your own tiny footprint.

LEAD BY EXAMPLE

I used to be the activist who drew attention to the fact that our oceans are full of plastic and dolphins are dying. The message had a repelling effect: instead of drawing people in and inspiring them to change, it freaked them out and they were gone. I noticed that whenever my girlfriends and I approached people for our Save the Mermaids education non-profit, we were able to break the ice by teasing that we were mermaids or explaining an allergy to plastic. So, I changed. Once people are chuckling and telling me that I'm not in fact a mythical being, I know I'm in. I explain that the oceans are filling with plastic and I've been sent by the merpeople to figure out why humans are so obsessed with the stuff. This also makes it fun for me to talk about the same depressing stuff again and again.

Another highly effective angle is purely to lead by example — with grace, positive vibes and solutions in tow. If you show up to the local cafe with your own cup, make casual convo in the check-out line about the discount you get for bringing your own cup. This is wholly different to shaming others for not bringing a cup, which can come through in your body language without you even uttering a word. That negativity won't encourage folks to jump on board. They'll only feel bad about themselves and, in order to rid themselves of the negative emotions, they'll avoid the entire situation. Fail.

If you go to a party, try bringing your own cup. It's likely you'll be the only one doing this. This makes you interesting. People may comment on your cup. There you go: now you can talk dolphins and turtles or whatever inspired you to dump plastics for good.

The more we show how easy, beautiful and fulfilling the plastic-free lifestyle is, the more appealing it becomes to others. This lifestyle is creative and enriching, not a horrible chore.

THIS IS NOT A SACRIFICE

We're rewarded with presents, encouraged to buy gifts for our loved ones' significant events, and this conditions us to think we are satisfied and fulfilled when we buy things. On the contrary, shopping does more to stimulate feelings of need than satisfy them. We find ourselves wanting new and wanting more. The process of cutting out plastics fosters our awareness and paves the way to living a more connected and authentically fulfilled life — with less stuff.

The truth is, all of the plastic-packaged stuff is part of an illusion constantly being sold to us. We've been brainwashed into believing that packaged food, drink and other products are superior to what we can make at home. And indeed, these things might be more convenient for us, since they're already made and processed full of preservatives so they won't go bad, but this is what the big brands are counting on. They're hoping you value your time over your health and happiness. This is where I invite you to reflect deeply on what's important to you.

If you hear yourself talking about not having time to prepare your own nut milk or make your own insect repellent, ask yourself: is this a story? Is this something I tell myself to avoid trying something new? Do I use this reasoning in other parts of my life? What relationships do I tell myself that I don't have time for? What activities do I tell myself that I don't have time for? Are any of them likely to be good for me, but I rule them out because they'd require too much energy from me?

If it's a question of energy, let's look deeper at the benefits of quitting plastics. For example, when we eat poorly, we have less energy. Most plastic-packaged food is crap. When we prepare our own food, our senses turn on and our stomachs begin digesting as we're cooking, so our bodies function better, extracting far more nutrition than if we merely order food and eat it on the couch. We also burn kilojoules making the food because we go outside to pick the herbs and we walk to the market. These small bits of effort, which only add minutes to the task, contribute to our quality of life. They give us more energy.

If it's a question of time, then how do you value this precious commodity? Is it quantity or quality? Are you capable of enjoying your down time or are you too sick, tired and stressed? If you had three more hours in your day, would you simply try and cram more work or activities into those hours?

Is it possible that we've been conditioned to go quickly, to be stressed, so that when someone asks, 'How are you?', we automatically answer with a sigh, 'Busy! But okay!' And, if so, is this less of our own choosing and more a result of the society we live in? Are we sucked in to the external pressures to succeed, to buy new stuff, to look good, to appear happy and put together, regardless of whether it's true? To be busy because it makes it look like we're on track to something important?

Perhaps we're less committed to being stressed and busy than we think. Perhaps we have more options and all we need is to be shown another way. A way out of this incessant cycle that, in the moment, is neither satisfying nor healthy. And since this moment, right now, is all we ever have, should we be putting more energy into achieving quality in each and every moment? Would that be better than managing our time as if it were part of an ever-diminishing store of moments required for performing an ever-growing number of tasks?

My belief is that we can achieve heaps and not be stressed. We don't have to stop working towards our goals or quit our jobs. Quitting plastics is just like committing to a meditation practice or a yoga routine. We can easily convince ourselves that we don't have time for the 30 to 60 minutes it takes for these practices. Yet, when we do them, it clears the mind and regulates emotions and invigorates the body. We become more present, we find our attention easier to focus and we're more efficient in everything we do. How would we not have time for something that makes us highly productive and effective across the board?

This is how I think of the minutes added onto my day to carry out my plastic-free living tasks. There's no longer the question of whether I have time for this. Because I know that I'm making choices that enhance my life in ways that the Western culture I was raised in rarely considers.

If I choose only what serves me well, I cannot use the Western approach to calculating time. Instead, I factor in my mental health, my emotional well-being, my physical health. What's going to make me happier? What's going to fuel my body in a lasting, positive manner? What's going to keep me emotionally balanced and stable? What's going to inspire joy and enhance my connection to myself, to nature, to others? These are the things I care about.

My time is bloody important. It's so important that I often choose to slow down to enjoy it more. And to intentionally challenge the programming that I need to be doing more, moving faster, achieving more. I bring this mindset to the tasks that take a little bit more time than just buying the plastic-packaged version. When I'm soaking nuts and seeds. Chopping fruit to be frozen for smoothies. Foraging for herbs in community gardens. Washing clothes by hand. Planting aloe vera everywhere I can. Chatting with elders. Playing with children. I'm not watching the clock tick down.

My practice is to stay present. My practice is to make choices that's aren't solely for right now, for today, for my convenience and to reduce time. My practice is to make choices that are in alignment with the world I want to live in and my values. And if the cost is a few minutes for blending and straining oats for milk or walking outside to pick rosemary, I practise absorbing that with grace and ease.

Shopping guide

Different shopping scenarios present different plastics challenges. Here are my tips for navigating the following five shopping scenarios.

THE AVERAGE SUPERMARKET

Unless you have excellent access to farmers' markets and/or bulk food stores, you'll most definitely find yourself in supermarkets. It's essential to have a game plan or else you could easily be overwhelmed by the immensity of plastic packaging on every single shelf.

To start with, stick to the outside aisles, where the fresh produce is kept. In the middle of the store is all of the overly processed, plastic-packaged crap that isn't good for you. All of it has been scientifically designed to taste good and trick you into thinking it's delicious or nutritious. In the long run, we're not looking after ourselves if we're mainly eating from the inner aisles of the shops. Also, anything refrigerated is going to be closer to fresh, and thus a healthier option!

If you come across produce such as spinach or cherry tomatoes and wish you had a little bag to contain them, head to the mushroom section and grab a paper bag. If the mushroom section doesn't have these, try the bakery. Failing that, ask the cashier. If no paper bags exist, you're entitled to ask the manager, why not! Share your preference for less plastic in their store. Being vocal in this situation is so important. You're a customer, and if they want your business, they'll listen. The more people who speak up, the more this message will get through to the people who can make change. Be polite and patient and suggest solutions.

You will build the habit of bringing your own reusable bag and then the habit of putting your cloth produce bags into your reusable bag, so everything you need is all together and you're ready to shop. Cloth bags play a leading role in helping reduce the deforestation associated with the production of paper products.

If you forget your reusable bag, walk around the store looking for a cardboard box that contained food that has now been displayed. Pack up your goods in this box.

Where possible, buy things in glass jars with metal screw-top lids. You can reuse these as containers to store dry foods and leftovers at home.

If you fancy shopping from the deli section, you may also wish to bring clean jars. Hand them over at the counter to be filled up with olives or pre-made salads. If the attendant is unwilling to do this for whatever reason, ask them to wrap your items in the paper they have behind the counter for meats and fish. Skip the plastic sticker if possible!

FARMERS' MARKETS

Track down the schedule for all of the farmers' markets in your area. At these, you'll likely be able to purchase freshly baked bread, in-season produce and hand-crafted delights. It's great to have the option to avoid mass-manufactured stuff produced by faceless machines or people in hygienic masks and go for treats handmade with love! Where possible, support the makers and creators who've taken care to craft up products. And enjoy their specialties!

Eating in-season foods is healthy for our digestion. It's easy to have confidence that this produce is organic because you can *ask* the person who grew it. What a concept! Often, we can convince ourselves we're out of time and miss the opportunity to connect with other humans; no wonder we then feel sad and lonely. Ask questions of your local growers and see them shine as they talk of their passions. Having a chat is healthy for the soul. Plus, this invites slowing down, which is good for the brain and good for the part of us that not so long ago lived in multigenerational communities. You can't go wrong here.

BULK SHOPPING

More and more shops are popping up that offer food and household goods for purchase in bulk. Generally, you can bring your own clean jars and bottles, which are weighed, then you fill them up from large containers — of rice, seeds, oils and dishwash detergent etc. The shops often have paper bags available, but ideally you provide your own containers. Once you fill them, they're weighed again. The weight of the empty container is subtracted so you pay only for the contents. It's for this purpose that I keep *all* the jars that come into my home. I love buying pickles and olives and Dijon mustard in glass containers with metal screw-top lids. I can easily repurpose all of these to store my bulk foods.

Be sure to ask where the foods are coming from and use your best judgement to determine whether or not the source is reputable. It's also worth asking how much plastic is used in the shipping of goods to the store.

Let's be real: not every bulk food store is directly connected to cashew trees and lentil fields. The bin contents come from the supplier, often in a large plastic bag or bucket sent to the store. As mentioned above, ask your store if the food is coming packed in plastic. If the food does come in plastic, find out the size of the bags the bulk food is arriving in. It may make more sense to you to order your own batches of certain bulk dry goods. You could either store them in your pantry or split them up with friends or like minded community members. Reuse and repurpose the plastic bags, unless you find a miracle recycler that you trust to do the job.

HONESTY BOXES AND OTHER ROADSIDE WONDERS

Here in Australia there exists a beautiful thing: the honesty box. A tiny wooden house sits on the edge of the road offering produce such as fruits, veggies, honey and seedlings. You pull your car over, have a look at what's on sale, and pop your coins into the box in exchange for what you choose. I am in love with this form of community trade. Poetic in its regenerative nature, preventing food waste and enabling a spirited, spontaneous stop on your travels. Keep your eyes peeled for roadside sellers if you're visiting new places. In different countries, this is often where you can find plastic-free snacks like salted nuts or spiced corn! These stops have led to some of my favourite travel experiences.

Plastic and social justice

Plastic pollution is just as much a social injustice as it is an environmental injustice. When China, which for many years had accepted the contents of the Western world's recycling bins, famously banned all plastic trash imports in January of 2018, the global waste market began to panic.

Top trash exporters like the USA, UK, Germany and Japan started flooding Southeast Asia with their waste. Thailand, Malaysia and Vietnam had to scramble to set up restrictions for the waste coming in and now much is being sent to Indonesia. But some of the new recipients cannot efficiently manage their own waste, let alone such a colossal volume of imported stuff. Off-loading trash to countries without sufficient management systems or processing plants in place is inhumane.

The trash doesn't break down for 1000 years, but that doesn't mean it stays put. It leaches toxic chemicals into the groundwater. Plastic waste blows into the waterways, polluting the local ecosystem. Sometimes the people get rid of it by burning it, which releases toxic gases that cause serious diseases, or by dumping it in rivers or out at sea.

At sea, plastic smothers the coral reef, kills the wildlife who mistake it for food, and makes its way onto the dinner plates of the local people via their seafood diet. It breaks up — notice the difference in language: it doesn't break down into the earth like a banana peel, it breaks up — into irretrievable microscopic bits that further pollute the water, air and soil.

Not just whales and turtles but people are suffering at the exponentially mounting plastic pollution resulting from our species' negligent overconsumption. The global North made single-use plastics a status symbol that brands capitalised on, and now markets are flooded with plastic shampoo bottles, food packaging and single-serve sachets and consumers cannot even remember what they did before plastics. Humans are referred to as consumers instead of just people! What is the solution? If the wealthy nations got us into this mess, are they responsible for getting us out? Probably.

The governments, the corporations and the privileged citizens of these wealthy nations will need to rise to the challenge to slow and cut off the flood of plastics into the global marketplace. Just as they made plastic convenience a status symbol, it's now time to reverse that and make natural, compostable packaging and homemade recipes cool again.

PLASTIC PRIVILEGE

If we assess the socio-economic status of most humans on the planet – or even the country we live in – cutting back on plastics isn't an option. The most affordable products – food, drink, cleaning products, personal care products – are packaged in plastics. Also, plastic-packaged food is sold at petrol stations, corner markets, liquor stores – these 'foods', or processed edible substances, are incredibly accessible. So, if someone only has one shop in their area and it happens to be full of plastic items, they're limited in the choices they can make. If someone is struggling to make ends meet, the cheapest items are what go in the shopping trolley, regardless of their packaging. Large families with many mouths to feed and bottoms to be diapered have to make decisions less from an ethical or environmental perspective and more from a place of necessity. That is not necessarily because they aren't aware of the impact of plastics on human health or environment, but because it's the only option. Most people would choose an alternative if it were available.

If you have the resources or privilege to make the change, this is your chance to help influence a social movement and economic shift. By using less plastics, we can assert our demand for less plastic packaging, alternatives to plastic, acceptance and allowance of reusables, refill systems and repurposed items.

This isn't just about quitting plastics, it's about working in solidarity to withhold our money and exert our social capital against this particular material, now that we're finally awake to our extreme over-consumption.

In terms of what one person can do to make a difference, quitting plastics is relatively simple. It's certainly not the only change one can make to meaningfully reduce human impact on our precious planet, but it's a good start.

Quitting plastics is a privilege. The zero-waste movement is elitist. Not everyone will have access to bulk food stores or farmers' markets near where they live. Plus these options are often quite expensive, putting them out of reach for most people who value eating this way. Some folks will literally only have the option to buy plastic-packaged food products for their groceries. Additionally, plastics aren't the priority when the pressure is on to feed the family or complete all of the work required.

With that said, those of us with the resources and awareness to make the changes should definitely make the changes. I suggest we should be reverently grateful for our privilege, and not waste it: use it for all it's worth. For the next few years, try to fly less, drive less, eat zero animal products to save the climate from warming beyond repair. If we can, we should choose to live a simpler life in the short-term so that we have a long-term. Consciously invest in organic food, bulk foods, reusable items, sustainable brands, natural clothing, recycled materials.

Every dollar we spend is either hurting or helping the environment and humanity. We must use our privilege beyond our personal gains, to support the collective benefit.

To clarify, I am not suggesting we shop more and buy more stuff to lead an environmental lifestyle. In fact, we must remain quite savvy around 'eco' products as frequently these are just another thing manufactured and not necessarily better for the planet – there is no regulatory body enforcing 'eco' claims, after all! We do not need to buy a reusable bottle, we can simply repurpose our kombucha bottle or purchase a second-hand bottle. There are plenty of products already in circulation; we don't need new stuff. That said, I do understand that if you invest in a product that really works well and that you love, you are more likely to use it and remember it. However, when we are faced with organic over non-organic, the better choice for our health is organic and the better choice for our planet is organic – this is because we are supporting farmers who are making the effort and going to the expense to distribute fewer pesticides. That means there are then fewer foreign chemicals absorbed into the food and the surrounding ecosystem where the food is grown.

When we are faced with making our own or buying packaged, we can try our best to make our own. The ingredients we need to make our own would best be purchased from local growers in reusable cloth bags or jars. The jars could be repurposed from food we bought, and the cloth bags could be sewn from repurposed fabric or in bulk from fairtrade suppliers that will refill and reuse their packaging.

I have found such satisfaction in living simply, and it started with a desire to create less waste. We will create less waste if we simply buy less stuff. We can do this if we focus our energy on finding fulfilment in our connection to nature, in our relationships, in our passions and hobbies. Let us consciously slow down. Let us watch the ways of nature, so that we may reconnect. Instead of rushing or reacting, let us be humble and learn. Let us remember.

In order to save the world, we must first come back to her. This connection will empower us deeply. This earthing will give us deep roots and deep wells of strength and understanding to make and sustain the necessary changes.

Quitting plastics is a relatively easy switch for the privileged. But we're the folks who've most likely been consuming at unsustainable rates. It seems like a fair move. For the most part, I'm eternally optimistic and idealistic, and I realise that lots of people quitting plastics isn't going to stabilise the mass consumption of the global North.

We need large-scale systemic change. We need governments to make and enforce stricter legislation. We need so many things. We need all the help we can get to reverse the impact of our disposable lifestyle, so any effort is in the right direction and our individual efforts do add up. Do not underestimate the impact of a small action.

Not only do these actions reduce the pollution on the planet. But you never know who is watching and being inspired by your efforts.

OUR CHOICES MATTER

Plastics is but one of many pressing issues in our world. It's easy to feel overwhelmed and helpless in the face of things like melting Arctic ice, increased incidence of natural disasters, intentional burning of ancient rainforest, human trafficking, overfishing … the list goes on.

I recommend reading Joanna Macy's work and channelling frustration into positive action. We all have to start where we are and do what we can within our capacity. At least with plastics, we can focus on our own impact. We can clean up our own trash cans and feel good knowing that our plastics aren't being shipped off to villages and communities without the consent of those residents. Little by little, these choices add up. And make a big difference.

HUMBLING OURSELVES FOR THE JOURNEY

Quitting plastics is a gateway. It opens the door. It is a manageable first step on a sustainability journey. Just as recycling makes us more open to other environmental commitments, so does reducing our plastics. Simply by bringing our own coffee cup or making our own hummus, we become more open to other environmental campaigns and ideas. People tend to resist change, especially when their comfort feels threatened.

The more we can show how easy and rewarding it is to reduce our use of plastics, the more people will join in and identify with the environmental movement. This is important because now more than ever, we have to curb our consumption of resources and regenerate our stressed planet. The atmosphere is saturating with greenhouse gases and the planet is overheating. We can make these changes now, when we feel inspired to make gradual shifts that enrich life. If we wait to make these changes, we may have less comfort as the timeframe for transition narrows.

Humility will serve us in this transition into collective action. The time for the ego has passed. Working together, sharing resources, looking after each other. We have technology to connect us to more people across the globe and communicate ideas faster. This age of awakening works if we stay open and humble. We cultivate humility so that we're always open to change and growth. To step outside into the rain and feel the wetness on our skin. To feel the chill in the air as a season changing instead of rushing to fix the discomfort of coldness. To drink as much water as we need, but wash with less than we're used to. To honour the energy that's gone into the food consumed at each and every meal. To remember we are but a flash in the planet's lifetime, and work towards a positive legacy. To strip back the convenience we have become so accustomed to. To make peace with and let go of some of the comforts and the cushy lifestyle that have been embraced by the masses and now overshoot the planet's resources. Humility will guide us through this.

CONFRONTING OUR CONSUMPTION

After quitting plastics for a month, we can become savvier shoppers and more conscious consumers. A month of a self-imposed limitations set on our purchasing creates more mindfulness when we shop, buy things, consume. We've broken the habit of impulse purchases or buying the items merely because of brand-name recognition or persuasive marketing printed on their packaging.

This can be a catalyst for us to buy less plastics. It causes us to regain some agency. We stop being herded in and out of shopping centres by the ads, coupons and marketing messages we're barraged by daily, sometimes hourly. Buy more! Do less yourself! Convenience! Ease! Be more beautiful! Skinny! Successful! Efficient! This product is the only way to achieve this!

Large multinational corporations literally spend billions to understand our psychology and what we care about, then create products and marketing to manipulate us into buying their stuff. It's sick and twisted and we all participate in it willingly. Until we don't!

How to deal with apathy

Now that you're on a crusade to save the world, you may be outraged by unconscious plastic use and — worse — conscious plastic use! There'll be some people who don't care in the slightest and will brandish single-use plastic in front of you just to annoy you.

How to deal? Humour is my favourite. My approach is to playfully tease them.

If this feels like wasted energy, begin with deep breaths. Remember you were once an oblivious plastic-user yourself. This person is unlikely to join the team if you react to their apathy or provocation with aggression or force. Stay calm and collected. Lead by example without forcing anyone to join you. Make it look good. Continuously offer opportunities to join your low-waste lifestyle and efforts. They may refuse 1000 times; they may cave once!

Read your audience and choose the argument that resonates with their values: environmental impact; whales with bellies full of plastic; how plastic leached into our food from cling wrap and plastic packaging sheds microplastics, contributes to depression and decreased mental health, cancer, heart disease, infertility, obesity and premature aging. They might launch into a story about surfing with plastics in Indonesia, or their cousin who couldn't get pregnant or some other personal anecdote. If you can help them relate to this far-reaching multifaceted catastrophe, you can make it personal and they may be more open to the discussion. And if all else fails, give them the finger.

Some people will try to argue that the impact of just one person does not matter. Show them the YouTube clip of the straw stuck up the turtle's nose. Ask them if they can prove that straw did not belong to them. We cannot know where our trash will end up and what will happen to it. Every little bit we refuse adds up and makes a difference.

TRAFFIC LIGHT SYSTEM

Here's a helpful tool I learned from Kat, a lovely gal who attended my Whale Shark Retreat in Western Australia.

Know where your energy and time is best used. One way of doing this is keeping the traffic light system in your mind when engaging with people. We have limited energy and we want to ensure that our efforts are having the most impact possible.

Green — people who are already a 'Yes' within the movement. No need to convince them of anything, recruit them to your campaign or help get them involved in a local organisation.

Yellow — these people are so worth our time. They are on the fence. They are curious, unsure of what to think and very open to suggestion.

Red — very hard to even engage in meaningful conversation. Red lights are often argumentative and a firm *no*. They require a strategic, thoughtful and patient approach. Keep setting a good example and being positive. Over time, they're likely to wear down into a changeable yellow light.

2

NOURISHING FOOD

Recipe list

Our wrestle with convenience

The most common roadblock for those embarking on the plastic-free path is food packaging. Our edibles mostly come in weather-proof packaging so they can last a long while on the shelves. That suits people who prefer to minimise shopping trips. We go to one big store to collect all that we need for a few weeks. Consequently, we get large quantities of things that are packaged so they don't go bad in humidity or become vulnerable to bug infestation. This makes it seem impossible to quit plastics, as in every aisle, products of all categories are packaged in the ubiquitous material.

Let's have another look at this behaviour. Does it make sense to buy *everything* from one store? Items that are manufactured, packaged and shipped from all over the world?

What happened to supporting local and regenerative programs? Is taking the most convenient path — focusing on our own comfort — more important? When millions of people take the easy way out, what are the consequences? Perhaps in the short term we save time and maybe money by shopping at one store. But when you factor in all the costs, our planet is bearing the long-term burden.

PLASTIC PACKAGING, EARTH POLLUTION AND POOR HEALTH

While we may be comfortable right now, much of the world is not. Around the globe, non-biodegradable trash is building up. Plastic finds its way into water systems that are often inadequate. It may have been casually discarded or illegally dumped or carried on the wind. It's picked up by currents then gathers in places like the Great Pacific Trash Gyre. Many poorer countries are living among waste dotted with labels from Western brands.

There are massive health implications as our world fills up with to non-biodegradable plastic. In some cases, poor countries accept our plastic recycling — so we feel clean — but their disposal practices may include burning the plastic, thereby generating high levels of air toxicity for the citizens of those nations, and ultimately for the planet. The plastic that pollutes our waterways is breaking up into microscopic bits, entering the food chain, causing irreversible deformities and genetic mutations. These are just some of the negative side-effects when plastic packaging ends up as trash.

I began avoiding plastic-wrapped foods for these reasons. The more I read about the negative impacts on our own health, the more my choice was reinforced and my resolve to be vocal intensified.

'The more clearly we can focus our attention on the wonders and realities of the universe about us, the less taste we shall have for destruction.'

– RACHEL CARSON, *SILENT SPRING*

Cut out plastic with BYO

We've all got to eat and drink, and the BYO tactic is for when you're out and about. Bringing your own reusable containers and utensils, so that you don't have to purchase a single-use plastic item, is probably familiar to you.

Rather than clank and clatter as you walk around with a bag full of silverware, cups and bottles, bring a napkin to wrap your reusables. More and more lightweight and easy-to-transport options are popping up, but there's no reason to break the bank. Go with what suits you and what you like using. I like using mini teaspoons with adorable artwork on the handles. The more you treasure the item, the more you'll use it and not lose it!

CLEAN IT ASAP

Don't let your reusable container or cutlery sit for ages without being washed. Tackle this as soon as you can. If possible, rinse it with water before putting it back in your bag. This prevents food from crusting on, which is especially important for straws. If you bring your own reusable straw, suck some water through and give it a good clean out before putting it away.

Eating wisely

Instead of listening to our bodies, we've come to trust and rely on nutritionists, doctors, diet books, food pyramids, food blogs and random promoters in grocery stores and supermarkets. And — perhaps weirdest of all — we trust the claims made on the food packaging, as if they were from Grandma holding out a fresh-baked pie, rather than a multinational profit-driven company with a priority to sell products. We overthink and underthink our food choices, often at the same time. Many of us don't even see food anymore; we're just calculating gluten, sugar, probiotics, carbs and calories. Some people do this with a reasonably good understanding, but mostly we allow ourselves to be easily swept up with new diet trends and superfoods.

No one really knows what we should be eating. So strange. If we can connect with and develop a closer relationship to our bodies, we have a chance at serving their unique and ever-changing needs.

Extracting plastic from my life has created a more meditative and conscious relationship with food. I cannot simply grab whatever lines the shelf; I have to be intentional, plan ahead and be flexible.

RETURNING TO THE ANCIENT WIDSOM

When I realised that cutting out plastics ruled out most options available at the stores, I knew I was making a commitment to sourcing and preparing most of my food myself. I searched for some baselines to guide my eating.

This led me to Ayurveda, a 5000-year-old natural and holistic approach to life that is rooted in India's Vedic culture. Studying Ayurveda rewarded me with a methodical approach to connecting with my body and honouring my needs. It helped me to notice the signals my body sends and understand what was needed. It taught me to nurture my body based on the seasons, my predisposition and what was happening in my life. Instead of treating symptoms, I addressed the cause with nourishing love and a change in diet or lifestyle. Often, the best medicine is hot tea, meditation, sleep, water or massage. Pure and cleansing, simple and divine!

This study informed my experimenting in plastic-free alternatives and recipe design. With access to such rich, deep wisdom and ancient texts guiding my hand, I was empowered to spice and stir and share the abundance of healing.

Below you will find two sets of food rules that helped shape my approach to eating. Following these rules will not only create harmony in the body but will also allow you to enjoy a balanced and peace-loving lifestyle.

AYURVEDIC FOOD RULES

* Eat only when hungry – you want to have enough digestive fire, or agni, to get the most out of your food.
* Don't eat if stressed out or upset – you won't properly digest or absorb nutrients.
* Eat while sitting in a calm and comfortable place – not while driving or walking.
* Keep good company and only discuss pleasant matters.
* Eat the right quantity. Ayurveda recommends that your meals be no larger than what you can hold with your two hands cupped together.

* Don't eat until stuffed – stop at two-thirds capacity or if you have a burp!
* Eat quality food – seasonal, local, organic produce.
* Eat warm, unctuous (juicy or a little oily) meals – these are easier to digest.
* Do not eat incompatible food items together in the same meal: for example, fruit digests fast, so it can disrupt digestion when paired with other foods.
* Avoid cold drinks with meals; they'll slow down digestion.
* When you eat, be present and eat slowly, chewing and tasting.
* Eat at regular times to help honour the body's natural rhythm.
* Give enough time between meals to generate hunger.
* Avoid eating 2–3 hours before bedtime.
* Take a walk after meals.
* Enjoy the food you eat!

MICHAEL POLLAN'S FOOD RULES

I love the simple and succinct philosophy of Michael Pollan's fabulous book, *Food Rules: An Eater's Manual*. It's based on just seven words: 'Eat food, not too much, mostly plants.' The first two words are very important. 'Eat food' means to eat real food – vegetables, fruits, wholegrains. It follows that you avoid what Pollan calls 'edible food-like substances', which of course means all the processed stuff sold as food. That's exactly the sort of produce that's packaged in plastic – not super-vibrant fuel for your body. Plus it pollutes the planet – you do the math!

This is Michael Pollan's advice for day-to-day shopping and eating:

* Don't eat anything your great-grandmother wouldn't recognise as food.
* Stay out of the middle of the supermarket. Real food tends to be on the outer edge, near the loading docks, where it can be replaced if it goes bad.
* Don't eat anything with more than five ingredients or ingredients you can't pronounce.

* When you eat something with 15 ingredients you can't pronounce, ask yourself what those things are doing there. Pollan is not a fan of things like portable yoghurt tubes.
* Don't eat anything that will not eventually rot. Pollan cites honey as a rare exception. Things like Twinkie bars, which never go bad, are not food.
* It isn't only what you eat but *how* you eat. Pollan recommends that we always leave the table a little hungry. He points out that many cultures encourage people to stop eating before they're full.
* Families have traditionally eaten together, around a table and not a TV, at regular times. It's a good tradition. Enjoy meals with the people you love.
* Cut the snacks.
* Don't buy food where you buy your petrol. In the US, 20% of food is eaten in the car. It isn't a healthy habit to get into.

Sourcing our food thoughtfully

Currently, an estimated 20–40% of our individual environmental footprint is related to our diet. We can reduce our footprint by buying mostly locally produced fresh wholefoods, like fruits and vegetables. I understand that this is not available to all: as with everything in this book, put energy into what is doable for you.

At the rate our population is growing, not all of us can have our own piece of land to grow food, so the dream of raising chickens and tending a veggie patch isn't attainable for all. It would be ideal to all be a part of a community that grows food together, shares resources and trades goods. The most earth-supporting way of life is still revealing itself to us as our planet and cultures shift. For now, I encourage anyone fortunate enough to have access to a patch of dirt to grow as much food as possible.

There are other things we can do now: shop at farmers' markets, trade with our neighbours and community members, and do our best to support dry goods from responsible sources. This is a lifestyle interconnected with nature. We do best when we know where our food comes from, who grows it, what it's sprayed with. Also, we nurture relationships within our community as we diversify our food sources. Maybe the beekeeper needs another spot to keep an apiary. Or you discover a repair shop at the local markets where you can bring a broken appliance or a ripped pair of trousers. The plastic-free lifestyle invites connection. It invites a curiosity and respect for natural systems, cultivation and regeneration of land for growing plants for food and medicine. The abundance of nature is truly astounding. All we have to do is support the systems that regenerate land for today and tomorrow and the future food supply. This is basic logic. The added benefit is living in harmony with nature. Romantic, poetic, deeply satisfying.

EAT PLANTS, NOT ANIMALS

According to the US Government's Environmental Protection Agency, in 2010 agriculture contributed 24% of global greenhouse gas emissions, and livestock alone is responsible for 14.5% of global emissions each year! Our species used to enjoy meat sparingly, like a Sunday roast or at a celebratory feast. Now it's so cheap, it's served three meals a day. How did this shift occur? Through clearing forest to raise cattle and, in many countries, to grow corn, soy and other feed crops, even though cattle have evolved to eat grass, not grains. They get fatter and make their producers more money with corn and soy.

Apart from the many associated losses — of biodiversity, wildlife habitat, the sequestration of carbon that trees do, soil quality (from the trampling of hooves) — the negative impacts of livestock farming include covering feed crops in synthetic fertilisers — often made from petroleum! — and the application of pesticides. More of this is discussed on my website www.iquitplastics.com and my podcast, The Mercast.

One of the best things we can do for the planet is stop eating animal products. If your body craves meat, feel that and try to feed it plant proteins. If it still craves meat, try to reduce your consumption to once a month. The more animal products we all eat, the faster our planet will heat up and kill the majority of life it currently sustains. Including us.

BUY WHAT YOU NEED

According to the UN Food and Agriculture Organization, globally 30% of food is wasted across the supply chain, contributing 8% of total global greenhouse gas emissions. If food waste were a country, it would come in third after the United States and China in terms of contribution to global warming. Australia and the United States are both in the top five countries with the highest rate of food wastage in 2019.

Food is either spoiled in transit or thrown out by consumers in wealthier countries, who typically buy too much and toss the excess. In a world where an estimated 805 million people go to bed hungry each night, that is disturbing in multiple ways, not least of which is the environmental cost of producing all that food for nothing.

It's estimated that if wealthy countries could cut down on food waste over the next three decades, this could prevent more than 70 billion tonnes of greenhouse gases from being released into the atmosphere. Next time you feel frustrated by the lack of environmental action from governments or corporates, remember that this is something all of us can do to help reverse global warming and at the same time feed more people, increase economic benefits and preserve threatened ecosystems. It boils down to making conscientious decisions to purchase what we intend to eat and eat what is purchased. Embrace 'ugly food' — fruits and vegetables that are blemished and not perfectly shaped but are perfectly delicious and nutritious. Properly store, use and share leftovers. Compost your food scraps so they don't contaminate materials that could be recycled or end up in landfill where as they break down they'll emit methane and contribute to the greenhouse gases warming our planet.

Part of re-evaluating our shopping routines is becoming more conscious about what purchases we make, where we make them and how long bought food items last. If you buy less stuff, less will go bad. Use what you have and manage your produce to keep it fresh. If any of it starts to go bad, compost it immediately to avoid it spoiling the rest.

Be choosey about what you buy in bulk. If you buy too much of something and it goes off, then everyone loses, and that includes the environment.

COST

Buying dry goods in bulk is usually a cost-saver in the long term but it does involve an initial outlay of cash. If it doesn't fit with your budget or if doing a long drive for the shopping trip is a headache for you, consider teaming up with others. Buying in bulk together and having a roster to do the shopping offers many benefits: fresh food at attractive prices, the chance to build relationships with like-minded legends, and you only have to do the shop in person every once in a while.

If your bulk items come in large plastic bags, return them in person or mail them back to the supplier ready for when you purchase your next batch. Of course, you'll need to first call the supplier and make sure they'll work with you on such an exchange. If they refuse, see if you can find a use for this plastic around your home or use it for purchasing bulk items from another supplier.

Managing fresh produce

When you eat real food, you buy a lot of fresh produce. Make sure you always wash your produce. Try diluting a splash or two of apple cider vinegar in a sink of water and allow all of the fruits and veggies to soak for 5 minutes, stirring and scrubbing if you like. Not only will this remove excess dirt and even pesticides, but it will also help them last longer by preventing mould.

TIPS FOR KEEPING PRODUCE FRESH

* Keep bananas away from your other produce, as they create some of the highest amounts of ethylene gas. (Ethylene gas is produced naturally by fruits and vegetables in the ripening process.)
* Put your herbs and stemmed greens in a glass of water, like flowers in a vase. They last longer and look beautiful!
* If you won't be using herbs for a while or if you have larger leafed greens, like spinach or rocket (arugula), wet a clean thin dish cloth or paper and loosely wrap the greens. Place them in a bowl or Tupperware container in the fridge.
* If your carrots go soggy, put them into a glass of water equal to their length; they will absorb the water and firm back up!
* Keep potatoes and apples together in a cool, dry place, but not in the fridge – apples keep potatoes from sprouting.
* Store onions separately! Once you cut into an onion, or if you have excess chopped onion, keep it sealed in a container. Onion is absorbent – hence the age-old remedy of using onion as a poultice to draw out toxins. It does the same in your fridge! Never eat unwrapped onion that has sat in the fridge.
* Store unripe fruits and veggies – like pears, peaches, plums, kiwis, mangoes, apricots, avocados, melons and bananas on the counter. Once they're ripe, move them to the fridge. Banana peels will turn dark brown, but this won't affect the flesh.
* If fruit becomes over-ripe, chop it up and store it in a container in the freezer. Later, blend up for a smoothie.

* Cut the top off your pineapple (and plant the top: more about this below). Store the pineapple fruit cut side down to redistribute the sugars.
* Tomatoes should stay at room temperature, away from sunlight to avoid spoiling them. Be sure not to store your tomatoes in plastic, as this will trap moisture and increase the likelihood of spoilage.
* Keep your fridge clean! Leftover residue or mould spores can increase the spoilage of all the food in the fridge.
* Don't store fruits and vegetables near a gas stove. Natural gas has been shown to speed up ripening as it's like the natural ethylene gas fruits and veg produce as they ripen. The same goes for the heat or smoke from toasters, kettles, sunshine, incense or candles.
* To keep cut apples, avocados or guacamole from turning brown, spritz with a little lemon juice.

PLANT YOUR KITCHEN SCRAPS

Grow your own garden for free by planting what you'd throw away!

Here's a run-down on what you can plant and from what stage. (Of course, do research to optimise results for your climate and season.)

FRUIT

* Pineapple: cut the top off. Peel back the leaves at the base, exposing the pineapple's neck. Put in jar of water until it sprouts little white roots. Then pop in the ground. She'll fruit in a few years.
* Papayas, cucumbers, lemons, melons, apples and cherries: scrape out the seeds and plant them. Even peaches can grow from their seed! Be patient; some take a few years. But it's so worth the wait! Try to only use seeds from organic produce as non-organic fruits often contain non-germinating seeds.
* Rinse tomato seeds, allow to dry, find some suitable soil and plant them in a pot. Once the sprouts are a few centimetres tall, transplant them outdoors to a full-sun plot.

VEGGIES

* Potato: cut in half, allow to dry overnight then transfer to the soil with eyes facing up.
* Pumpkin: spread out the seeds in a sunny area then cover with soil.
* For lettuce, spring onions, leeks, fennel, bok choy, celery and even coriander (cilantro): cut off all tops, leaving about 5 centimetres (2 inches). Pop into a glass and add 1 centimetre (2.5 inches) of water or enough to cover the base. Change the water every few days. Once you see regrowth, or after 5–7 days, transfer to the soil. Note that bok choy doesn't thrive with too much full sun.
* Cabbage: place leftover leaves in a bowl with a small amount of water. Position the bowl in a sunlit area. Change the water every two days. When roots and new leaves appear, transplant to soil.
* Red onion: cut off the edges of the onion to make a square around the roots. Plant directly in soil and cover with 2.5 centimetres (1 inch) of soil.
* Sweet potato: place in a jar of water – one end will stick out. Roots will grow below, and leaves will grow above. Plant it outside to grow more sweet potatoes. Note that unlike the common potato, sweet potato leaves are edible and healthy!
* Capsicums (bell peppers) and chilli peppers: scrape out the seeds and plant them in soil, either in a pot or in the garden. Place them in a sunny area to grow.

HERBS, RHIZOMES AND FUNGI

* Basil, coriander (cilantro) and rosemary: strip the leaves from three-quarters of the stems then place the stems in jar of water in a spot that's sunny but not too hot. Change the water every day. Transplant to a 10-centimetre (4-inch) pot once the roots are 5 centimetres (2 inches) long.
* Ginger: take a fresh hand of ginger, break off a piece and plant it outside in soil or in a small pot in indirect sunlight. It will grow new shoots and roots. When ready to harvest, pull up the entire plant, remove what you want and replant to keep it growing.
* Mushrooms: remove the mushroom cap or head, place the stalks into the soil, covering everything but the tip.

How – and why – to love composting

Composting is one of the most important things you can do for the environment. According to modelling by Project Drawdown, a non-partisan organisation that promotes a climate-safe future, worldwide implementation of composting could cut emissions by over 2 billion tonnes over the next 30 years. Food waste left to decompose in landfills (an anaerobic process) releases methane, a greenhouse gas that's at least 28 times more potent than carbon dioxide. Food waste that's composted not only produces far less methane (because it's an aerobic process) but it can be used as a fertiliser, improving soil health and productivity.

Globally, more and more high-density population urban centres where people live in small spaces are developing innovative composting systems, like the one practised in New York City. People living in apartments can collect food scraps (apart from meat and dairy) in their fridge then drop them off at one of the many conveniently located collection points. Using high-tech aerobic processes, top-quality compost is produced.

For the householder, without messy food waste in the garbage, it won't smell, plus there's much less to dispose of. This, in turn, makes it viable to move away from placing household waste in plastic trash bags. If you're not there yet, consider placing newspaper in the bottom of your bin. You can then carry your small bin to your wheelie bin and tip it all straight in! Same amount of effort; far less waste without the plastic bag.

There are many home composting systems, starting from the basic dig and drop for those lucky enough to have a good-sized garden. Choose the one that suits your lifestyle. Depending on how many people there are in your household and how much plant waste your kitchen generates, you may find the cultivation of earthworms that feed on food waste works best for you. If this is the case, you'll have a constant supply of liquid fertiliser for your garden and pot plants. At the garden centre, you'll be able to walk briskly past those plastic bottles of popular soil-enhancing nutrients.

KEEPING YOUR SINK-SIDE COMPOST HAPPY AND CLEAN

Try to empty your kitchen compost each night before you go to bed. If you get the little bucket emptied regularly, it won't smell or attract bugs. Build this into your dishwashing routine. Once all the dishes are clean, empty the compost, return to the full sink of what is by now dirty dish water and give your bucket a good rinse and scrub. If you have a hose outside by your compost dump, that can be a good time to give the bucket a rinse too.

Using the recipes

To save ink, the words 'organic, GMO-free, locally sourced, plastic-free, bulk-bought, Fairtrade' won't appear in front of every ingredient in every recipe. Do your best to tick all those boxes when shopping. Be mindful of the carbon emissions caused by food transportation (or 'food miles'), and if some ingredients I recommend using are getting flown and shipped around the world, please get experimental with the recipe and instead try using something that grows locally in your region.

PREPARATION

It can be tempting to buy pre-made food packed in plastic, especially if you're working a lot or feeling the pressure of shortening hours of daylight. Resist! Get creative and prepare in advance. Involve the family in food prep as bonding or chores or whatever works. Make large quantities on Sundays and freeze them in Tupperware containers. Have potlucks with friends!

Making your own food in your own kitchen with wholefood ingredients is going to keep you and your household out of hospital later in life.

MOSTLY VEGAN

I believe cutting out animal products is an important way to lessen our impact on the planet. All of these recipes are 'beegan': that is, vegan plus bee products, like honey.

As new information comes to light, I do change my opinions and practices, but currently I feel that supporting local beekeepers by purchasing their honey supports the European Honey bee population, which is currently in rapid decline.

By purchasing from a local human and not a faceless mass honey-producing corporation, I can ask specific questions. Also, I can usually return my container to the beekeeper for refill or reuse, which makes this a circular exchange where no packaging waste is created.

Nourishing food recipes

STAPLE FOODS

Plant milks, breads and dressings are the sorts of thing you'll find yourself whipping up frequently. Creating routines around these everyday staples is key to making this lifestyle switch sustainable. Additionally, you'll find that replacing processed, packaged foods with homemade versions will have a positive impact on your energy levels, quality of life and general well-being. Practise these recipes now, while you have the energy and interest! Experiment and perfect them to your taste. Then this practice can flow into your busy life easily.

So often, bread comes packaged in plastic to stay 'fresh'. But can you even pronounce all the ingredients the manufacturers slip into that dough, much less digest them? Whether you have gluten or wheat intolerances or not, I highly recommend avoiding the stress of wondering if bread is good or bad, and see how making your own feels in your body.

Taking charge of what we put in our bodies is incredibly empowering. Be accountable for the pollution you personally create. Be healthy and clean in your body and on your earth.

Almond Milk

I love having fresh, homemade nut milk in the fridge ready for hot chai and turmeric lattes. Many nut milks on the market are packaged in cardboard lined with plastic. This is certainly not being recycled — it's too costly and difficult to separate these resources. Also, if you've ever made your own nut milk, you know it goes bad in under a week. So what the heck is in the shelf versions of nut milks to keep them edible? Eek!

Get in the habit of soaking at night and squeezing in the morning, and you'll have plenty of milk for your tea and cereal. In this book, you can find recipe ideas for using the nut meal you are left with after milking your almonds.

---

2 CUPS ALMONDS, SOAKED OVERNIGHT, DRAINED AND RINSED

2–4 DATES, PITTED

3 CUPS WATER

½ TEASPOON GROUND CINNAMON

Blend all ingredients until creamy.

Strain through mesh nut milk bag into a clean bowl. Carefully squeeze out all of the liquid.

Pour the nut milk into a bottle and store in the fridge for up to 5 days. A few days in, shake and smell before use to ensure it's still good.

Tip: Leftover almond meal can be used immediately in a raw dessert recipe or even as a body scrub. To save for later, spread it in a pan and place it in the oven on low heat until the remaining moisture evaporates. You can use this almond meal for gluten-free baking.

———

Oat Milk

This is the most sustainable plant milk because oats are less taxing on the land than most nuts. If you can, soak your oats overnight: not only does this soften the oats but it helps remove the phytic acid that inhibits proper digestion. Technically, oats are gluten-free; however, most are processed in plants with wheat, so the likelihood of contamination is too high to claim GF.

---

1 CUP ORGANIC OATS (ROLLED, STEEL CUT, OR OAT GROATS)

3 CUPS PURIFIED WATER (PLUS EXTRA FOR SOAKING)

1 PINCH SEA SALT

1–2 PITTED DATES OR 1 TEASPOON RAW HONEY (OPTIONAL)

⅛ TEASPOON VANILLA EXTRACT OR GROUND CINNAMON OR GROUND NUTMEG (OPTIONAL)

Cover the oats in purified water and leave to soak for at least 30 minutes or up to 12 hours.

Drain and rinse the oats well. You want to wash them thoroughly so that your oat milk isn't gooey. Discard the rinse water.

Put the drained oats into a blender, add 3 cups of purified water, the sea salt, sweetener and spices, if using. Blend for 1–2 minutes.

Strain in a cheesecloth or nut milk bag to remove pulp. Use excess pulp as fibre for smoothies or to make oatmeal treats.

Store milk in a jar in the refrigerator and use within 3–5 days. Shake well before using.

Cashew Cream

This will keep in the fridge for up to a week. Mix with a fork or blend again if the cream separates.

---

1 CUP RAW CASHEWS, SOAKED OVERNIGHT, THEN DRAINED AND RINSED

1½ CUPS WATER

1 TABLESPOON PURE MAPLE SYRUP

½ TEASPOON VANILLA EXTRACT

Blend cashews and water until creamy.

Add maple syrup and vanilla extract and blend for another minute.

Store in the fridge.

Tip: This can be nice in your smoothies, or whip up a thicker batch and serve with fruit and granola for dessert.

Sunflower Seed Kefir/Yoghurt

This recipe makes just under a litre (a quart) of delicious, rich non-dairy yoghurt drink that offers protein and friendly gut-loving flora. This is a three-stage process that requires 8 hours to soak the seeds and an additional 6–12 hours to ferment before blending into kefir. Worth it.

---

2 CUPS RAW SHELLED SUNFLOWER SEEDS, SOAKED 8 HOURS IN WATER, THEN DRAINED

2 CUPS WATER

1 TABLESPOON MAPLE SYRUP OR RICE MALT SYRUP

1 TEASPOON VANILLA EXTRACT OR GROUND VANILLA BEAN

1 TEASPOON GROUND CARDAMON

Place the soaked seeds in the blender and add just enough water to cover them. Blend until creamy.

Add more water if necessary to achieve desired consistency.

Pour into a glass container, cover with a clean towel.

Place in a warm (not hot) position. Leave to ferment for 6–12 hours. If you don't have a warm place, wrap the container in a towel or scarf and leave for 24 hours or until thick and bubbly. It will ferment quickly if you are in a warmer climate, and you can also leave longer for a more tart taste.

Stir in the rest of the ingredients.

Enjoy as a gut-health drink, a vegan substitue or as a little parfait topped with fruit.

Store sealed in a jar in the fridge.

Gluten-free Seed Bread

I learned this gem of a recipe when I first moved to Byron Bay. The gorgeous girls I lived with were always whipping up delicious treats, and this easy, tasty loaf was a staple. It's delicious with anything. Try toasting it. If the loaf proves too delicate for the toaster, let a slice rest on a non-stick frypan on the stove instead.

1½ CUPS BUCKWHEAT (SOAKED OVERNIGHT, THEN DRAINED)

1 CUP SUNFLOWER SEEDS, SOAKED AND DRAINED

½ CUP PEPITAS, SOAKED AND DRAINED

¼ CUP ALMONDS (OR ANY NUTS), SOAKED, DRAINED AND GROUND

½ CUP FLAXSEEDS

1 TABLESPOON SESAME SEEDS

2 TABLESPOONS CHIA SEEDS

4 TABLESPOONS PSYLLIUM HUSK

1 TEASPOON SEA SALT

1½ CUPS WATER

3 TABLESPOONS COCONUT OIL, MELTED

1 TEASPOON SLIPPERY ELM (OPTIONAL)

Mix all ingredients together in a large bowl.

Line a loaf tin with coconut oil or baking paper (I always wash and reuse baking paper until it's no longer coated, then I compost it). Pour your seed mix into the tin, cover with a cloth and leave overnight (or 4 hours, if you're despo for bread in your life).

Bake in the oven at 160°C (320°F) for 1 hour or until the top has browned and crisped.

Remove from the oven, flip the loaf upside down onto a wire baking rack then pop back in the oven for a further 30 minutes to an hour.

Remove and allow to cool for at least 1 hour. Store in the fridge.

_____

VARIATIONS

Garlic Rosemary Bread: stir in 3 minced cloves of garlic and the leaves of 3 sprigs of rosemary.

Sweet Breakfast Bread: stir in 1 tablespoon maple syrup, ½ teaspoon ground cinnamon, ½ teaspoon ground cardamom and ½ teaspoon ground nutmeg.

Ayurvedic: stir in ½ teaspoon chilli flakes, ½ teaspoon ground cumin, ½ teaspoon ground turmeric, ½ teaspoon ground black pepper and 1 teaspoon cumin seeds.

Rosemary and Almond Vegan Paleo Bread

Make your morning nut milk and then repurpose the meal for this incredible bread, which tastes as sensational as it smells. Many of my savoury dishes include the hearty flavour of rosemary. It's good to include a pinch of rosemary in your cooking as it's a natural anti-inflammatory with many medicinal properties. Try to cultivate a bush or two, whether indoors or out! Rosemary is easy to grow and can survive a bit of frost in winter, although it wouldn't last a full freeze over.

2 CUPS ALMOND MEAL

¼ CUP PSYLLIUM
HUSKS

¼ CUP CHIA SEEDS

¼ CUP FLAXSEEDS

½ CUP RAW WALNUTS/
HAZELNUTS, CHOPPED
+ 2 TABLESPOONS
EXTRA FOR TOPPING

3 TABLESPOONS
ROSEMARY LEAVES
(¾ OF THEM
CHOPPED)
+ EXTRA FOR TOPPING

2 TEASPOONS
HIMALAYAN SALT

1½ TEASPOONS
BAKING POWDER

4 CLOVES GARLIC,
CRUSHED

3 TABLESPOONS
FRESHLY GROUND
CHIA

9 TABLESPOONS
WATER

¼ CUP FRESH,
HOMEMADE NUT MILK

1 TABLESPOON OLIVE
OIL

Preheat the oven to 190°C (375°F).

Lightly oil the bottom and edges of a standard bread tin or line tin with baking paper.

Combine the almond meal, psyllium husks, chia seeds, flaxseeds, chopped nuts, rosemary leaves, salt, baking powder and garlic in a large bowl and mix with a wooden spoon.

Mix the chia and water and leave to sit for 5 minutes or until it is the texture of raw egg yolk. Combine with the nut milk and olive oil.

Stir the liquid into the mixture and combine thoroughly.

Spoon into your bread tin. Sprinkle with walnuts and rosemary.

Bake for 30 minutes or until a toothpick inserted in the centre of the loaf comes out clean. If you have used very fresh nut meal, you may need to give it 20 minutes more in the oven!

Remove from the oven and allow to cool, then slice and serve.

Beer Bread

This is not gluten-free, but it's full of healthy protein-rich seeds. And beer! People are always intrigued by recipes that use unexpected or surprise ingredients, especially when they get to drink the remaining beer!

---

3 CUPS SELF-RAISING FLOUR

¼ CUP TOASTED SUNFLOWER SEEDS

¼ CUP CHIA SEEDS

1 TABLESPOON GROUND CUMIN OR FENNEL SEEDS

2 TABLESPOONS HERBS (E.G. BASIL, THYME AND/OR ROSEMARY)

350 ML BEER

¼ CUP COCONUT OIL, MELTED

1 TEASPOON HONEY OR MAPLE SYRUP

Preheat the oven to 180°C (350°F). Grease a bread tin with oil or line it with baking paper.

Mix all the dry ingredients then slowly pour in the beer, melted coconut oil and honey. Stir well.

Spoon the mixture into a bread tin then bake for 50–60 minutes or until a toothpick inserted into the middle of the loaf pulls out clean.

Allow to cool, then slice and enjoy!

Vegan Bone Broth

This is a nutritious, gut-healing vegan alternative to bone broth. The vegetables listed below will give you a terrific result. You don't need every single one of these: just pop in as many as you have. Maybe try saving your veggie off-cuts in a sealed container in the fridge. A wide variety of veggies will boost the nutritional goodness.

---

12 CUPS (2¾ LITRES) FILTERED WATER

1 TABLESPOON COCONUT OIL OR EXTRA-VIRGIN OLIVE OIL

1 RED ONION WITH SKINS, QUARTERED

1+ GARLIC CLOVE, SMASHED

30 G DRIED WAKAME SEAWEED (IF YOU CAN FIND THIS IN BULK; YOU MAY BE LUCKY ENOUGH TO SOURCE SOME FRESH FROM A MARKET OR A FISHERMAN)

1 FINGER FRESH TURMERIC WITH SKIN, CHOPPED

1 CHILLI PEPPER WITH SEEDS, ROUGHLY CHOPPED

1 THUMB-SIZED PIECE OF GINGER WITH SKIN, ROUGHLY CHOPPED

1 CUP GREENS SUCH AS KALE OR SPINACH

3–4 CUPS MIXED CHOPPED VEGETABLES AND PEELINGS (I USE CARROT, RED CABBAGE, MUSHROOMS, LEEKS AND CELERY)

½ CUP DRIED SHIITAKE MUSHROOMS

1 TABLESPOON PEPPERCORNS

2 TABLESPOONS GROUND TURMERIC

1 TABLESPOON SEA SALT

BUNCH OF FRESH CORIANDER OR OTHER HERB OF YOUR CHOICE

Add everything to a large saucepan and bring to a boil. Simmer with the lid on for about an hour.

Once everything has been cooked down, strain the liquid into a large bowl.

Serve fresh garnished with herbs. Store in the fridge in a large jar or freeze.

Few-ingredient Dressing

Too often the dressings for our salads come packaged in plastic bottles. When they contain sugar, preservatives, dyes, thickeners and other ingredients you'd never find in your grandmother's garden, it is a nasty reminder of the reckless profit-driven behaviour of both corporate manufacturers and the corporate supermarkets they sell to. We can collectively disempower such companies by not purchasing their plastic-packaged products and instead voting with our dollar to support local, organic producers of food that is made with intention. Dressings may seem like a small way to participate in this plastic boycott, but when you see how easy these are to make, you will feel the 'power to the people' potential!

---

1 SPOON OLIVE OIL

1 SPOON SEEDED MUSTARD

1 SPOON SOY OR TAMARI SAUCE

1 SPOON LEMON JUICE

1 SPOON TAHINI (OR YOUR CHOICE OF NUT BLENDED WITH WATER)

Whisk with a fork until well mixed. Adjust to taste.

Tip: Depending on how much you need, choose the appropriate size of spoon. To dress one salad, use a teaspoon; if feeding a tribe, use a tablespoon. I never measure precisely. I merely taste test and adjust along the way. These are my favourite ingredients to mix for dressings, I try to use an oil or a sauce or a juice and thicken it with the tahini or mustard. Whatever's in the fridge is fair game for the dressing. Have a go!

The versatility of nuts and seeds

Nuts and seeds are the original superfoods. They can be used in a huge array of meals, either as the star (like in a nut roast or chia pudding) or as a quiet background dressing or sauce. Combinations of nuts and seeds make fabulous topping for dishes such as salads and crumbles, or sprinkled on top of your morning porridge. Dairy-free milks and cheeses are almost impossible without them, and they're essential ingredients for tart bases, bliss balls and crunchy granola. Not to mention, nuts and seeds are a great little snack, raw or seasoned, in combinations or on their own.

In addition to their versatility on your plate, nuts and seeds have an astounding array of nutritional benefits, and make up an important part of dietary requirements, particularly for those of us who avoid meat and dairy! They are best enjoyed in moderation: just five or ten at a time are enough for the day. This is important to bear in mind when we are cutting dessert or serving nut-based cheese portions. If we are having a nut milk latte, nut cheese spread on a sandwich, a nut-based pasta sauce and nuts in our dessert, that is a lot of fat – even if it is healthy fat. If I am super active and doing a lot of cardio, I can manage. If not, I will take my coffee black and blend a strictly veggie spread and/or pasta sauce.

Additionally, while nuts and seeds can be a terrific source of nutrients, in raw form they can be hard for our bodies to digest because they contain an enzyme inhibitor called phytate that blocks digestion. This is how they have evolved to protect themselves in nature! Try soaking, sprouting or toasting them to help your gut get more benefits. Not only will this process make digesting your nuts and seeds easier, but it will increase the number of vitamins and proteins your body absorbs from these super foods!

Soaking nuts and seeds replicates the natural germination process where a plant grows from a seed. Sprouting nuts or seeds activates and multiplies nutrients (particularly Vitamins A, B, and C), neutralises enzyme inhibitors and promotes the growth of vital digestive enzymes. You can sprout seeds and nuts and even grains and beans! The method is the same; it's just the soaking time that varies.

It's worth noting that truly raw seeds and nuts will sprout; however, if you soak nuts that have been pasteurised and irradiated, they will 'activate' and therefore be easier to digest and have increased nutrition – but not physically 'sprout'. This is a good way to test if your supplier is truly raw or not! An opportunity to ask more questions, help drive transparency up the supply chain, and help them clarify in labelling their product.

To sprout sunflower seeds, fill a large, clean glass jar one-third of the way with sunflower seeds. Add a pinch of sea salt. Fill the rest of the jar with filtered water. Cover with thin, breathable clean cloth and tie twine around the jar to keep the cloth in place and keep bugs out of your sprouts! Soak for 30 minutes to 2 hours. Drain and rinse well with fresh water. You will not soak these seeds again. Flip the jar upside down and set at an angle so that air can circulate and the water can drain off. Leave for about 8–12 hours, then rinse with cool water. Drain for another 8–12 hours. By now the seed has soaked up enough water to break its dormancy; it holds the magic of life and is an amazingly powerful food!

To toast, put a handful of nuts or seeds in a pan on low heat until golden, stirring often to avoid burning. If you prefer a sweet snack, for each cup of nuts or seeds, before heating toss them in ½ tablespoon of honey or maple syrup and 1 teaspoon of salt.

Tamari Almonds will remain fresh for weeks if stored in an airtight container in the fridge. Soak 2 cups of whole raw almonds for 12 hours then dry on a towel and toss in 2 tablespoons of tamari. Bake in an oven at 180°C (350°F) for 12 minutes, then shake the tray and return for the oven for another 5–10 minutes, removing when they're crispy.

To make high-protein Spicy Seed Mix, soak your choice of shelled seeds overnight, dry on a towel, then toss in a bowl with ½ teaspoon ground turmeric, ½ teaspoon ground cayenne, ½ teaspoon ground cumin and 1 teaspoon olive oil. Spread on a baking tray and bake in an oven at 180°C (350°F) for 15 minutes.

Meals

We are all different. That is the truest aspect of nature. All things are connected, nothing exists alone, and nature thrives where there is biodiversity. This book is an invitation to experiment your way into the adventure that is a plastic-free life. This is not another trend that encourages us all to adopt the same behaviours — buy the same things, eat the same, look the same, act the same. *No.* Instead, try some of these starting points and find what works for you. Unique, independent, sovereign, beautiful you.

Rather than presenting a comprehensive selection of recipes that could potentially overwhelm you, I've picked through my hundreds of recipes and chosen my favourites plus examples that hopefully will support you on your journey. I figure that if I can show you some principles, give suggestions for ways you can adapt them to suit your tastes and situation, you'll have a lot of fun crafting your own style. If you find yourself wanting more, there are plenty more recipes on my website, iquitplastics.com, and my channel, youtube.com/c/plasticfreemermaid.

Cutting out single-use plastics from daily life usually starts with altering our takeaway food habits and bringing reusables. The next obstacle is avoiding food packaging. This requires us to get a little crafty in the kitchen. The delicious and healthy recipes on these pages will sustain and support your choice to quit the plastics.

Breakfast

What I love about breakfast is that you can pretty much justify anything you crave — pancakes and waffles included — adapting to what your body needs or your routine dictates. Personally, I don't get hungry until later in the day, after my morning workout, so I end up having more of a brunch. Here are some suggestions for creative ways to start your day without requiring plastic-packaged cereals or shelf-stable chemically preserved milks.

On a summer's morning, it's hard to beat starting the day with a colourful fresh fruit salad. Chop up a selection of delicious fruits, place in a bowl and enjoy! You can add toasted seeds or nuts for added protein, or granola to make it heartier.

This could be to do with my brekky inching closer to lunchtime, but I think salad is too delicious to be left out of our morning nourishment. Wash and toss together mixed greens. If you have access to kale, be sure to massage it with a small amount of oil or else it will not work with your taste buds or digestion. Make a simple dressing — just lemon juice can be enough. Toast some seeds and sprinkle over roast veggies or grate them raw into the salad and enjoy! Add ¼ avocado, salt and pepper, spices, maybe leftover grains from last night's dinner — whatever you feel like to make it yummy and filling.

Chai Chia Pudding

This dish nails it if you're after a quick, easy, delicious and gourmet breakfast. It could even be a crowd-pleasing dessert. It's protein rich and filling, and perfect for catering for a group or when travelling; you can work miracles with a can of coconut water and a few scoops of chia. To 1 part chia seeds, add 4 parts liquid, stir and leave overnight to set. In the morning, add fresh fruit or other yummy toppings, such as granola or chopped nuts. Your choice of liquids includes coconut water, fruit juice, plant milk, plain water with spices or, as in this recipe, tea. For a creamier pudding, make the chai with ½ cup water and 1 cup plant milk.

1¼ CUPS WARM CHAI
(SEE PAGE 130)

¼ CUP CHIA SEEDS

1–2 TABLESPOONS
MAPLE SYRUP

1 TEASPOON VANILLA
EXTRACT

SLICED BANANA

1 TABLESPOON
TOASTED SUNFLOWER
OR PEPITA SEEDS

Strain the chai into a jar, add the chia seeds and stir.

Leave in the fridge overnight or until the pudding is solid.

Remove from the fridge and give a nice big stir. Add the maple syrup and vanilla and stir again.

Top with the sliced banana and sprinkle with the toasted seeds.

Mix again and enjoy.

Super-chunky Cluster Granola

This granola makes a great gift! Find your cutest jars, bake up some delicious chunky granola and fill the jars with your sweet treat. Tie some natural twine around the jar for a lovely decorative touch.

---

1 CUP QUINOA FLAKES OR OATS

½ CUP SOAKED PEPITAS

½ CUP SOAKED SUNFLOWER SEEDS

1 CUP SOAKED HAZELNUTS/ALMONDS/ WALNUTS/PECANS, CHOPPED

1 TABLESPOON CHIA

1 TABLESPOON FLAXSEED

PINCH SEA SALT

3 TABLESPOONS COCONUT OIL

3 TABLESPOONS MAPLE SYRUP

1 TEASPOON VANILLA EXTRACT

½ CUP DRIED FRUIT

½ CUP LARGE FLAKED COCONUT

Preheat the oven to 160°C (325°F).

Mix the dry goods (not the coconut flakes or fruit) in a large bowl.

Add the liquid (the coconut oil will become liquid on a hot day; if not, heat it over a low temperature on the stove first). Stir well so the sticky liquid coats everything and the mixture can form into clusters. Allow to soak for 1 minute.

Spread evenly onto the baking tray. Bake for 20 minutes. Don't stir or you'll prevent clusters from forming!

Remove from the oven then spin the tray so the other side of the pan gets the heat from the back of the oven and the mix bakes evenly.

Return to the oven and bake for another 10–15 minutes, making sure the clusters don't burn. Once golden, remove and allow to cool in the tray without disturbing the clusters.

Add the dried fruit and coconut flakes. If you wish, you can toast the coconut flakes on the stove beforehand. Break off chunks and clusters and store in a jar with a tight-sealing lid.

Sweeten instead with ½ cup of a sweet spice or floral tea, like chai or orange. For this you'll need to bake the granola longer because it will be wetter.

Note: This makes a delicious topping for coconut yoghurt or a smoothie bowl. It's also a satisfying dessert, especially when served with some N'ice cream (see page 116)!

Sticky Date Porridge

When I first moved to Australia I was shocked that I had lived life without ever tasting Sticky Date Pudding. While the traditional version was full of white sugar, the healthy version is just as brilliant. After some experimenting, I was able to translate the dessert to breakfast as well. I love all oats but I particularly love mixed-grain oats. Buy or blend your own mixture of wholegrain rolled oats, barley, spelt, amaranth, rye, triticale, brown rice or quinoa flakes for a healthy, hearty bowl of goodness. Any leftovers can be stored cold and enjoyed as a 'soaked-oat pot' snack. Add chopped fresh or dried fruits to give new life. Make a big batch of this for the week; each morning, heat it up starting with a bit of coconut oil and ground cinnamon in the saucepan. Fresh oil and spices are the key to giving any leftovers fresh life.

1 CUP OATS (OR QUINOA FLAKES)

2 TABLESPOONS FLAXSEED

3 TABLESPOONS CHOPPED PECANS

5 FRESH MEDJOOL DATES, PITTED AND CHOPPED

1 TEASPOON ORGANIC VANILLA ESSENCE

½ TEASPOON GROUND CINNAMON

½ TEASPOON SEA SALT

1 TEASPOON MESQUITE POWDER

1 CUP WATER (OR NUT MILK IF YOU PREFER A CREAMIER PORRIDGE)

1 TEASPOON RAW HONEY OR MAPLE SYRUP

Place oats, flaxseeds, pecans, dates, vanilla, cinnamon, salt and mesquite in a small saucepan. Stir until mixed.

Pour in the water and stir well.

Increase the heat to medium and bring to a boil. Then reduce the heat and simmer.

VARIATIONS

Mango Turmeric Porridge: replace the mesquite powder, pecans and dates with the following:
1 teaspoon ground turmeric
pinch of ground black pepper
1 cup chopped mango

Peanut Butter Banana Porridge: replace the mesquite powder, pecans and dates with:
1 tablespoon nut butter
½ mashed banana
½ teaspoon ground nutmeg

Carrot Cake Porridge: replace the mesquite powder, pecans and dates with:
½ carrot, grated
1 tablespoon chopped walnuts

Stir in the honey or syrup. Serve hot.

Kitchari

This Ayurvedic dish is hot, spicy and unctuous and ridiculously simple to prepare. It's healing for the gut. It makes a yummy savoury breakfast. It can also be the basis of a winter cleanse — the counterpart of the summer juice detox. The cleanse entails eating this dish for breakfast, lunch and dinner for three to seven days. It gives your belly a break from cold or hard-to-digest foods. I like to prepare a large pot of Kitchari then, each day, transfer the amount required into a small saucepan — along with fresh oil and spices — and heat it up on the stove.

Note: If you tend to run hot and intense, avoid adding too much chilli or mustard seeds; it could make you speedier. If you tend to go slow and need a kick to get going, chilli and ginger are your friends.

Tip: The onions, garlic, ginger and tomato add depth to this dish; however, these can be omitted if you want something simple and cleansing that's incredibly easy to digest. It slides through your digestive tract while still being filling and nourishing. Unlike many other cleanses, this will support you through your everyday lifestyle, no matter how active you are.

---

1 TABLESPOON
COCONUT OIL

1 TEASPOON CUMIN
SEEDS

1 TEASPOON MUSTARD
SEEDS

½ ONION, CHOPPED

1 THUMB OF GINGER,
FINELY CHOPPED

1–2 CLOVES OF
GARLIC, CHOPPED

1 TOMATO, DICED

2 CUPS RICE

2 CUPS RED LENTILS

12 CUPS WATER

1 TEASPOON GROUND
TURMERIC

1 TEASPOON GROUND
CUMIN

1 TEASPOON CAYENNE
POWDER

½ TEASPOON SALT

½ TEASPOON PEPPER

1 TEASPOON FENNEL
SEEDS

CHOPPED FRESH
CORIANDER, TO SERVE

Spoon the coconut oil into a large saucepan on medium–low heat. Add the cumin and mustard seeds.

Once the seeds begin to pop, add the onions and stir for a minute. Add the ginger and stir for a minute. Add the garlic and stir for a minute, letting the flavours open up.

Add the tomato, pressing down into it with your spoon to release the juices. Stir thoroughly.

Add the rice and lentils and stir for one minute, allowing them to be coated in oil and spices.

Add the water, then the turmeric, cumin and cayenne and stir to mix.

Allow to simmer for 30 minutes, stirring every 10 minutes. As the rice and lentils cook, the mix should get thicker. Once thick and smelling delicious, taste a small spoonful, adjust the spices to suit and sprinkle with salt and pepper.

Enjoy your first bowl. You can garnish with fresh coriander (cilantro).

Store the rest in the fridge. When you want to heat up some of it, activate its healing qualities by putting a small teaspoon of oil in the saucepan, a pinch of mustard seeds and cumin and then adding the Kitchari. Stir well to heat up the Kitchari thoroughly.

Hero foods: small touches for a good day

Since incorporating Ayurvedic practices into my life, I start my day with meditation, a drink of hot lemon water then a stretch – sometimes for an hour or more, sometimes for just 20 minutes. Next, I massage myself with oil, from feet to shoulders, and take a shower to help the oil trap in the water's moisture. I brush my teeth, massage my face with oils suited to my facial skin and make a tonic. I might journal, or have a dance, or set intentions to design my day.

I find that choosing the right nutrition makes a massive difference to my mood and energy levels through the day, so here are my top tips.

LEMON WATER

Make your first drink of the day a cup of hot water with a squeeze of lemon juice. This primes your digestive tract and increases the metabolic rate. The minerals and vitamins found in lemon juice help maintain the pH of the belly, thus reducing heartburn or acid reflux. Additionally, it helps loosen any toxins trapped in your digestive tract. Definitely rinse your mouth with fresh water after the lemon water to save your teeth. Voilà, miracle morning!

PAPAYA

A serve of plain papaya is the best Ayurvedic brekky to get your belly working and metabolism ticking for the day. If you need something heartier, fill a papaya boat with chopped fresh fruit and granola. When you scoop out the seeds of the papaya, you could try planting them if you live in the tropics or eating a couple if you're having trouble with worms or parasites. Otherwise, drop them in the compost.

CHILLED BREKKY IN JARS

This is another great hack for the busy folks who struggle to make time for breakfast or who blank on what to make for a healthy meal. Prep your chia puddings and oat pots the night before. Or plan out your smoothies with cut-up fruits stored in the freezer.

OAT POTS

Soaking oats overnight in water or plant milk makes the grains easier to digest and gives us a head start when we wake up. I always add spices to aid digestion and chopped fresh fruits for their natural sweetness. Nuts and seeds are fabulous additions to tick the protein box. To make 4 serves of Spiced Oats, I combine 2 cups oats, 1 can coconut milk, 1 cup water, ½–1 cup chopped walnuts, 1 teaspoon ground cinnamon, 1 teaspoon ground cardamom and 1 tablespoon maple syrup (optional). In the morning I serve with chopped apple.

BREKKY BALLS (AKA BLISS BALLS)

If you have to lever yourself out of bed and hit the track pretty fast, it can be tempting to skip breakfast. Keep a bunch of nutritious, brekky-style bliss balls in the fridge. Drop a couple in a bag and you're good to go!

To make Turmeric Chai Brekky Balls, combine 12 soft pitted dates, 3 tablespoons coconut oil, 1 teaspoon of honey (or maple syrup; adjust quantity to your taste), 3 tablespoons almond meal, ¼ cup quinoa flakes (or oats), 1 teaspoon ground turmeric, a tiny pinch of finely ground black pepper, ½ teaspoon ground cinnamon, ½ teaspoon ground cardamom and 2 tablespoons coconut flakes. To give the final product a snowy coconut exterior, you could roll each ball in desiccated coconut.

SWEET POTATO – THE GLUTEN-FREE BREKKY SUPERFOOD

Cook up some sweet potato (or use leftover), add coconut cream and spices and mash to the consistency of porridge. Add toasted seeds or dried fruit to make it interesting. You could make a large batch and freeze it in breakfast-sized serves. To enjoy later, place in a saucepan with a bit of coconut oil and a pinch of fresh spices, and heat up gently on low–medium heat.

Lunch or dinner

There is more to mealtimes than the actual food. I think of breakfast as a peaceful meal to be enjoyed with the birds chirping and aromas of fresh black coffee and juicy ripe fruit. Brunch can feel social, light and joyous. As an entrepreneur, I often have to remind myself to step away from the computer and make time to be present for lunch. This essential meal energises me for the rest of the day. If I'm on my own schedule, I love an early dinner to prevent going to bed with a full stomach. But my favourite dinner is definitely a shared vegan potluck with friends. Truly, it is the most fun and delicious gathering.

As a lover of vegetables and all plant-based dishes, I offer the following recipes to inspire you to create protein-rich, highly nutritious, filling, healthy meals for yourself, for your friends and for a healthy future.

I group these meals together as they are fairly interchangeable. Depending on your food philosophy, you may prefer a heartier meal around midday and a lighter dinner. Regardless of what foods at what times best nourish your body, these recipes are some of my favourites. Ultra-delicious and plastic-free because the main ingredient is always simply a heap of fresh, local, organic veggies. When in doubt, just bake a bunch on a tray or grate raw into a salad! Veggies are always the best choice.

Zoodle Pad Thai

I've made my own pasta a few times with great success, but there isn't always the time to knead dough and hand-roll noodles. Plus, my belly always feels thrice the size after even a small bowl of flour pasta. Zucchini noodles are so easy, whether you have a 'zoodler' device or simply a reliable peeler to peel away long thin lengths for your fettucine slices. As for the sauces, they're yours to invent! This one is my go-to.

---

3 ZUCCHINIS

2 CARROTS

2 SPRING ONIONS

2 GARLIC CLOVES

1 RED CAPSICUM
(BELL PEPPER)

1 HOT RED CHILLI

A LARGE HANDFUL OF
GREEN BEANS

½ HEAD BROCCOLI

3 TABLESPOONS
PEANUT OIL (OR
OTHER HIGH SMOKE-
POINT OIL)

½ CUP MUNG BEAN
SPROUTS

Peel the zucchini and carrot into ribbons but keep them separate. Finely chop the spring onion and garlic. Cut the capsicum and chilli pepper into strips. Trim the green beans on an angle. Chop the broccoli into florets.

Put 2 tablespoons of the peanut oil into a pan and heat. Add the onions, garlic and chilli. Stir-fry (stirring constantly) until the spring onions soften and the garlic becomes fragrant. Transfer to a separate plate, leaving as much oil in the wok as you can.

Heat up another tablespoon of oil in the same wok – no need to wash it. Start adding the prepared veggies in the following order (leaving 1–2 minutes between each addition): broccoli, red capsicum and carrot ribbons. Stir-fry until cooked yet still crunchy.

Transfer the cooked vegetables to a large plate or bowl and keep warm.

¼ CUP ROASTED AND
UNSALTED PEANUTS,
POUNDED
IN A PESTLE AND
MORTAR

FRESH CORIANDER
AND LIME WEDGES, TO
GARNISH

SAUCE

5 TABLESPOONS
TAMARIND SAUCE

3 TABLESPOONS
TAMARI/SOY SAUCE

2 TABLESPOONS
MAPLE SYRUP (ADJUST
QUANTITY TO TASTE)

2 TABLESPOONS
WHITE VINEGAR

1 TEASPOON CHILLI
FLAKES

1 TEASPOON
HIGH QUALITY
PEANUT BUTTER

Mix together the sauce ingredients and pour into the bottom of the wok. Add the zucchini ribbons.

Return the stir-fried veggies to the wok. Mix everything well, stirring the entire time, for 1–2 minutes or until sufficiently warm.

Divide between two plates, top with sprouts and sprinkle with crushed peanuts and coriander. Serve with lime wedges on the side.

Lentil and Chickpea Falafels

I learned this beautiful recipe on The Big Island of Hawaii at the retreat space of my mermaid sister Kaia and her husband, Garrett. My visit coincided with a yoga teacher training course, so I met a number of bright shiny yogis. Occasionally, Garrett opened up the kitchen so they could whip up magic of their own. The wonderful Yana prepared this incredible dish and it's been a constant in my cooking repertoire ever since. Not only are these falafels baked rather than fried, you can make them from leftover beans, lentils, chickpeas, rice, hummus or even oatmeal!

---

1 CUP DRY RED LENTILS

2 CUPS WATER

1 CAN CHICKPEAS (GARBANZO BEANS), DRAINED AND RINSED

½ CUP SOAKED SUNFLOWER OR PUMPKIN SEEDS

2 TABLESPOONS CHOPPED RED ONION

2 GARLIC CLOVES, MINCED

JUICE OF 2 LEMONS

2 TABLESPOONS TAHINI PASTE

Preheat the oven to 200°C (400°F).

Place the red lentils and the water in a saucepan and cook on the stove on high heat for about 15 minutes.

While the lentils are cooking, combine the chickpeas, sunflower seeds, red onion, garlic, lemon juice, tahini paste, cumin and parsley in a food processor. Process until thick and not quite smooth. Add the flax meal and mix again to combine. Transfer this mixture to a large bowl.

Once the lentils are cooked, discard any excess liquid and stir into the chickpea mixture.

Sprinkle with salt and pepper, then stir in the sesame seeds, almond meal, spices and coconut flour and allow to sit for 5 minutes.

1½ TEASPOONS
GROUND CUMIN

¼ CUP CHOPPED
FRESH PARSLEY

1 TABLESPOON FLAX
MEAL

¾ TEASPOON SALT
AND PEPPER

1 TABLESPOON
SESAME SEEDS

1 TABLESPOON
ALMOND MEAL

1 TEASPOON
GROUND PAPRIKA

½ TEASPOON
TURMERIC POWDER

¼ TEASPOON
CAYENNE POWDER

½ TEASPOON
GROUND
CINNAMON

½ TEASPOON FINELY
CHOPPED CHILLI
PEPPERS

1 TABLESPOON
COCONUT FLOUR

¼ CUP COCONUT
OIL

Cover a baking sheet with foil or parchment paper, then lightly grease with coconut oil, using your fingers.

Using a large spoon, measure out about a palmful of the chickpea and lentil mixture and form a patty in your hand. For smaller falafel balls, use a tablespoon to measure out.

Once all the mixture is on the baking sheet, transfer to the oven.

Bake at 200°C (400°F) for 20–40 minutes.

Tip: To go the whole 9 yards when you serve, cut up some flatbread – allow 1 piece per 2 falafel patties. Open the bread and add a dollop of hummus on one side.

Sit the falafel patties on the hummus. Add chopped cucumber, carrot, tomato, avocado and massaged kale. Drizzle over a blend of tahini and lemon as sauce.

Veggie Coconut Curry

2–3 TABLESPOONS COCONUT OIL

1 TEASPOON MUSTARD SEEDS

1 TEASPOON CUMIN SEEDS

1 ONION, CHOPPED

¼ CUP GRATED GINGER

2 CLOVES GARLIC, MINCED

1–2 SMALL CHILLIS, CHOPPED (OPTIONAL)

½ TABLESPOON GROUND CUMIN

1 TABLESPOON CHOPPED FRESH CORIANDER

½ TABLESPOON TURMERIC POWDER

½ TABLESPOON CAYENNE POWDER

1 TEASPOON GROUND CINNAMON

1 HEAD OF BROCCOLI, CHOPPED INTO FLORETS

1 RED CAPSICUM (BELL PEPPER), SLICED THINLY

3 CARROTS, SLICED

½ HEAD OF CAULIFLOWER, CHOPPED INTO SMALL FLORETS

1 SWEET POTATO, CUBED

1 ZUCCHINI, CUBED

1½ CUPS CHOPPED KALE

1 BULB OF FENNEL, CHOPPED

1 CAN COCONUT MILK OR BLENDED FRESH MEAT OF COCONUT

RICE OR QUINOA TO SERVE

Heat the coconut in a large saucepan on medium heat. Add the mustard and cumin seeds.

Once they pop, add the chopped onion, stir and then add the ginger, garlic and spices, stirring all the while.

Add your vegetables and get them all nice and coated in the sauce.

Add the coconut milk and stir. Fill the can with water and add four to five cans of water to the mix, depending on how thick you want your curry.

Allow to simmer for 15–20 minutes or until the veggies are cooked.

Serve with rice or quinoa.

Desserts

Sweets seem often to come packaged in plastic — and contain heaps of chemicals too. Bad for the Earth, bad for us. Making your own desserts is a nice thing to do for your friends or family while simultaneously setting yourself up for success with plastic-free living and sticking to health goals.

Serving a fruit salad may sound boring, but it might be a welcome relief for those trying to watch their waistline! My favourite is slices of tropical fruits arranged artfully on a tray and garnished with edible flowers and leaves. If you're taking it to a shared meal, squeeze over some lemon or lime juice to keep the fruit from going brown.

It's amazing how addicted to white sugar most of us are. Once we come back to treats that are naturally sweetened with fruits and honey, we tend to really savour the flavour and find more satisfaction. As well as enjoying our sweets more, we crave less, reduce sugar addiction and reduce plastic trash. Get creative and have fun in the sweet department. And remember — all things in moderation. (Except laughter and vegetables.)

Peanut Butter Cups

I have fond memories of trick or treating at Halloween. I would stack the peanut butter cups and hide them like little chocolate treasures. The most prized of all the candy. I would trade large quantities of less-loved sweets for just one of these treats. Of course, now I baulk at the white sugar, preservatives, and mostly the individual plastic wrapping for each little candy. Thankfully, I created a delicious recipe for both 'milk' and 'dark' chocolate cups. Hope you enjoy them as much as I do!

First, master your favourite chocolate recipe. Decide what proportions of coconut to cacao you love. Then you can get experimental with other flavours and ingredients.

1 CUP COCONUT OIL

⅓ CUP CACAO

1 TABLESPOON MAPLE SYRUP + 1 TEASPOON FOR PEANUT BUTTER FILLING

1 HEAPED TABLESPOON PEANUT BUTTER OR ALMOND BUTTER

PINCH OF SEA SALT

Mix the coconut oil and cacao in a small saucepan on low heat, stirring until melted. Stir in the tablespoon of maple syrup.

Pour half of the chocolate mixture into a mini cupcake tin or chocolate mould, only filling halfway.

Place the tray in the freezer so the chocolate can harden.

In a small bowl, whip together the peanut butter and teaspoon of maple syrup.

Remove the chocolate cups from the freezer and smear the peanut butter onto the chocolate. Pop back into the freezer for 15 minutes or until chocolate has set.

If needed, reheat the remaining chocolate mixture to make it runny again. Remove the chocolate cups from the freezer and top each one with the chocolate mixture. Return to the freezer.

After 5 minutes, remove the Peanut Butter Cups from the freezer and sprinkle with sea salt.

Store in the fridge.

VARIATION

Dark Choc Peanut Butter Cups: Same recipe, but increase the cacao to 1 cup to make a darker, more bitter chocolate.

Salted Caramel N'ice Cream

I like how many folks have declared vegan ice cream to be called 'n'ice cream'. It's nice to animals and the planet! Just a quick plug for veganism: dairy cows and their manure produce greenhouse gas emissions that contribute to climate change. In fact, at the time of publication, the meat and dairy industry produces 60% of agriculture's greenhouse gas emissions. Loss of wild areas to agriculture is the leading cause of the current mass extinction of wildlife. Poor handling of manure and fertilisers can degrade local water resources and create poor water quality that stresses coastal ecosytems, including coral reefs. Unsustainable dairy farming and feed production can lead to the loss of ecologically important areas, such as prairies, wetlands and forests. So, best to avoid animal products if we can and inspire others to do so too, by making delicious plant-based foods to share.

We used to have beautiful vegan potlucks at my house in Byron Bay. Friends would all gather with an array of decadent dishes. On one occasion, everyone brought desserts. There were zero main dishes It was accidentally an incredibly indulgent gathering! Another time just a small cake was left for the last course to be shared among a large group. I was able to whip up some N'ice Cream to balance the dessert bowls in the time it took us to enjoy appetisers and mains.

This works beautifully with frozen bananas and coconut cream but is equally as delightful with any frozen fruits!

Let's be honest: you could easily just blend bananas into N'ice Cream and be deeply satisfied. For something a bit fancier, you could try variations such as soaked cashews, almond butter, spices, a little honey or maple syrup and some homemade plant milk. Cacao nibs, toasted coconut flakes and nuts make excellent toppings.

---

1 FROZEN BANANA	Blend.
1 TABLESPOON ALMOND BUTTER	Freeze for 2 hours.
1 TEASPOON MESQUITE POWDER	Blend.
	Freeze for 2 hours.
3 TABLESPOONS PLANT MILK	Blend.
¼ TABLESPOON HIMALAYAN SALT	Serve.
1 TABLESPOON MAPLE SYRUP	

Succulent Sorbet

This is one of my favourite versatile desserts: it can be repurposed again and again as a fancy thick shake or a breakfast smoothie bowl topped with granola. It's beautiful to serve this dessert garnished with some fresh passionfruit. I also love serving a scoop of this after dinner on a hot summer's night or having a lick after a long sunshine surf! Perfect at any time of day.

---

4 FROZEN BANANAS

PULP OF 2 PASSIONFRUITS (PLUS 1 EXTRA TO GARNISH)

1 TEASPOON CHOPPED FRESH GINGER

1 CAN REFRIGERATED COCONUT CREAM

2 TABLESPOONS HONEY

Blend all the ingredients except the garnish. Whiz until well combined.

Pop into the freezer for 2 hours.

Blend again and return to the freezer for 2 hours more.

Blend again, then top with passionfruit pulp and serve.

Snacks

Store-bought snacks usually come packaged in plastic. In order to avoid plastic, be prepared, plan ahead and make your own snacks. If you make one batch of each of these recipes, you'll have a delicious nibbly platter for a picnic or potluck dinner, and who doesn't love that! Surround bowls of dip with a selection of crackers and strips of fresh crisp veggies. To dress it up even more, add little clusters of chocolates and dried fruits. Fill in any blank space with one or two tall candles and local native leaves and non-fragrant flowers.

Beetroot Chippies

Root veggies are nutritionally superb for our bodies and they make fabulous chips when baked or dehydrated. This recipe works for eggplants as well. The key is to get a nice thin slice, using a sharp knife or mandolin.

---

12 BEETROOTS

½ CUP OLIVE OIL

2 TEASPOONS SEA SALT

Preheat the oven to 160°C (325°F).

Scrub the beets with a veggie brush, rinse with water and vinegar and cut off the tops. Use a sharp knife or mandolin slicer to slice the beetroots paper-thin. For slices this thin, there's no need to peel them first.

Place the beetroot slices in a large bowl and add the oil and salt. Toss well. (If using red and golden beets, place in separate bowls and divide the oil and salt evenly.) The oil coats the beets in preparation for baking, while the salt seasons and sweats the moisture out. After 5–20 minutes, the beets have released excess moisture and they're ready for baking at low heat. This helps their shape and colour.

Toss the beetroot again, then drain off the liquid. Arrange the slices in a single layer on baking sheets. Bake for 30–60 minutes until crisp but not brown. Test after 30 minutes and only bake longer if necessary. Remove the chips from the oven and allow to cool completely before storing in an airtight container.

Gluten-free Seed Crackers

These seed crackers are definitely a go-to snack to make on a weekly basis. It's great to have these yummy little protein-filled hits handy in the fridge for a healthy snack or to pull out if friends call around. These are easy to whip up and look fabulous on a nibbly platter.

½ CUP FLAXSEEDS

¼ CUP CHIA SEEDS

½ CUP SUNFLOWER SEEDS

½ CUP PUMPKIN SEEDS

¼ CUP SESAME SEEDS

1 TEASPOON FINE SEA SALT

1 CUP WARM WATER

Preheat the oven to 180°C (350° F) and line a tray with non-stick baking paper or grease a tray with oil. In a large bowl, combine all the seeds and salt with your choice of seasoning. Add the warm water and stir until well combined. Taste and adjust seasoning if desired. Allow the mixture to sit for 30 minutes or until all the water has been absorbed.

Pour the mix onto your baking tray, spreading with a large spatula or the back of your stirring spoon. Thickness should be no more than 0.5 centimetres. Score the mixture by lightly running a sharp knife along the sticky mix to create surface lines. This will make it easier to break into evenly sized crackers after cooking.

Bake for 30 minutes. Then remove the trays from oven, lift the baking paper out and flip the crackers over so that the bottom side bakes. If you're not using baking paper, use a stiff spatula to carefully lift one side of each crackers. It should mostly all lift up as a solid sheet.

Carefully turn the crackers over and return to the oven for 20 minutes more. If they're already quite dry, then leave them in for 5–10 minutes. This will depend on how thick the crackers were when they went into the oven. To test for readiness, tap the top of a cracker. It's done if it's solid, dry and brittle. If it feels spongy at all, pop it back in the oven.

Turn off the oven and allow to cool completely with the door open. This will make the crackers extra crunchy! If you are time-crunched, however, no prob: remove from the oven and break into individual crackers. This should be fairly simple if the mixture was scored before baking.

VARIATIONS

Cheesy Crackers: Add ¼ cup nutritional yeast, 1 teaspoon onion powder
Herbed Crackers: Add 1 teaspoon herbs, 1 teaspoon garlic powder
Spicy Crackers: Add ½ teaspoon chilli flakes, ½ teaspoon cumin, 1 teaspoon cumin seeds, ½ teaspoon black pepper

Hummus

I used to advocate for always whipping up hummus and bean dips from organic canned legumes. Then I learned that the cans are lined with plastic and even those that proudly claim to be free of BPA (Bisphenol A) are lined with another type of Bisphenol — every bit as dangerous to our health — I've gone back to soaking my peas and beans! Still, this is all about minimising our exposure, and sometimes canned beans are all I have access to.

---

1 CUP CHICKPEAS, SOAKED 24 HOURS, DRAINED AND RINSED

1 TEASPOON CUMIN

2 TABLESPOONS TAHINI

3 GARLIC CLOVES, CRUSHED

1 LEMON JUICED

¼ CUP WATER

100 ML OLIVE OIL PAPRIKA OR CHILLI FLAKES OR ROASTED CAPSICUM (OPTIONAL)

PEPPER (TO TASTE)
GARLIC (TO TASTE)
CUMIN (TO TASTE)

CORIANDER LEAVES TO GARNISH

Pop all ingredients into blender and blend until smooth.

Spoon into a dish and pour 1 teaspoon olive oil on top.

Sprinkle with a bit of pepper, garlic and cumin, and top with coriander leaves.

Note: Don't worry if you have hectic breath after eating food containing garlic, this is super healthy! It means your lungs are being disinfected during your smelly exhalation!

Cashew Vegan Cheese

Learning how to make cashew cheese was essential to my veganism and this recipe is suitable for inexperienced chefs. This cheese is a hit on its own, with crackers or spread onto bread for closed- or open-faced sandwiches.

---

2 CUPS RAW CASHEWS, SOAKED, DRAINED AND RINSED

2 TABLESPOONS NUTRITIONAL YEAST

JUICE OF 2 LEMONS

ZEST OF 1 LEMON

2–3 GARLIC CLOVES, MINCED

½ PINCH CAYENNE POWDER

½ TEASPOON SEA SALT

¼ TEASPOON PEPPER

¼ CUP WATER

Blend the cashews, yeast, lemon juice and zest, garlic and seasoning.

Scrape the sides down and continue blending, slowly adding the water. The mix will get thicker and more like hummus. If you prefer a thinner consistency, add more water, 1 tablespoon at a time, blending carefully.

Taste the cashew cheese, and add more salt, pepper or lemon according to your taste.

If you don't eat it all straightaway, spoon into a glass jar to store. Because of the lemon content, this will keep for a week in an airtight container in the fridge, but, like all food, it's best eaten when fresh!

Granola Bars

An easy, healthy, yummy snack for people of all ages.

---

1 HEAPED
CUP OF SOFT
(MEDJOOL) DATES
(ALTERNATIVELY,
SOAK DRIED DATES IN
WARM WATER FOR 30
MINUTES)

1½ CUPS OATS (OR
QUINOA FLAKES)

1 CUP CHOPPED NUTS,
SOAKED

⅓ CUP COCONUT
FLAKES

1 TEASPOON GROUND
CINNAMON

CHOCOLATE CHIPS
(OPTIONAL)

DRIED FRUIT
(OPTIONAL)

¼ CUP MAPLE SYRUP
OR HONEY

¼ CUP NUT BUTTER

1 TEASPOON VANILLA
EXTRACT

Blend the dates into small bits and place in a bowl.

Add all the dry ingredients and set the bowl aside.

In a small saucepan melt the maple syrup and nut butter on low heat.

Pour this into the bowl, add the vanilla extract and mix evenly.

Transfer into a 20-centimetre x 20-centimetre (8-inch x 8-inch) pan and press flat.

Bake at 160°C (325°F) for 20 minutes.

Remove and chop into bars.

Store in a sealed container in the fridge or – to keep for longer periods – freezer.

Drinks

We humans can go three weeks without food but only three to four days without water. We're composed of around 60% water; 71% of our planet's surface is covered in water. Yet, we take too much water, waste it, negligently poison water sources. Worldwide, 780 million people don't have access to safe drinking water. Our relationship with water must heal if our relationship with the planet is to heal.

All things are interconnected in this complicated planetary ecosystem comprised of micro-ecosystems that make it so diverse and wonderful. I also believe deeply in hydration for our health. To acknowledge our individual need for water is to acknowledge our collective need for water. Often when we think we are hungry, we are actually just thirsty or dehydrated. However, being able to quench this thirst is a luxury! So yes, let's make magical tonics and enjoy our hydration rituals. With intentional reverence for our fellow humans who are less fortunate and with great respect for this resource: while it falls from the sky, it seems to be growing scarcer as our pollution expands ever outwardly.

Sipping tea and hot tonics has been a staple for maintaining health for thousands of years across cultural and class lines. Hot water on its own is always going to be soothing and replenishing for the gut. If ever unsure, stick to that. But I invite you to cultivate the art of selecting spices and picking fresh herbs based on what your body needs. This entails developing a better understanding of plants and also a deeper connection to intuition and interpreting the messages being communicated from the physical body. If you're already super clued up on herbs, maybe start listening more to the ever-changing nature of your body. Maybe you know what your body needs, just not what the plants do! Please tune in to my online resources for more guidance and detailed info on all of this!

As always, I invite you to experiment. If you have herbs or edible flowers in your garden, gather these! Or source loose dried herbs at your local market or from someone in your community. Grind with a mortar and pestle, place in a tea pot and add boiling water. Let steep for 10 minutes.

Chai

I learned this recipe when I studied Ayurveda. I so enjoyed studying this rich ancient practice. We were in school all day listening to our professor move anecdotally through the course material. At 11.30am, we always took a break for tea. All students took a turn making chai. If you couldn't make chai, you wouldn't pass the course. The same went for the dahl we made at lunch.

Our professor was most particular about his chai. If it disappointed him in any way, he wouldn't drink it. And we had to think pleasant thoughts as we made it. One should never prepare food with a heavy heart or an afflicted mind; it's transferred to the food. I love that even in preparing the chai we meditate.

In Ayurveda, cow's milk is used. I tried to take my chai without cow's milk. My very strict professor reminded those of us with this request that we would be depriving our spiritual bodies of the metaphysical healing properties of milk. I tried to embrace the learning in its pure form and drink the chai to see if the impacts of dairy were felt. I felt heavy and lethargic. Not surprising. It's not as if this milk came from the dairy farms just half an hour's drive from our classroom, where happy cows frolicked in beautiful green pastures. No, it was in plastic sold at a supermarket. Not really your top choice for nirvana milk. Since then, I've tended to buy my own tea and I make my chai with coconut milk or oat milk.

5-CENTIMETRE (2-INCH) PIECE OF FRESH GINGER, CHOPPED

2 CINNAMON STICKS

1 TEASPOON BLACK PEPPERCORNS

10 CLOVES

6 CARDAMOM PODS

10 FENNEL SEEDS (OPTIONAL)

6 CUPS WATER

3 TABLESPOONS LOOSE BLACK TEA LEAVES

2 CUPS COCONUT MILK

Combine the ginger, cinnamon sticks, peppercorns, cloves and cardamom in a medium saucepan and add the fennel seeds if desired. With the butt of your wooden spoon, crush the cardamom pods to release the seeds and gently bruise all the spices.

Add all the water. Bring to a boil over high heat.

Reduce the heat to medium-low, partially cover the pan and allow to simmer gently for 10 minutes.

Add the black tea leaves then allow people who don't drink milk to take their cups of chai.

Add the milk and strain the chai into a teapot. Serve hot.

Turmeric Daily Health Tonic

If there was one thing I learned in Ayurveda, it was that a pinch of turmeric a day keeps the inflammation away.

---

1 TABLESPOON
GROUND TURMERIC

1 TEASPOON GROUND
CINNAMON

1 TEASPOON GROUND
BLACK PEPPER

½ TEASPOON
BICARBONATE OF SODA
(BAKING SODA)

1 TEASPOON GREEN
TEA POWDER

½ TEASPOON GROUND
LICORICE ROOT

½ TEASPOON FENNEL
SEEDS

½ TEASPOON GROUND
GINGER

½ TEASPOON GROUND
CARDAMOM

½ TEASPOON DRIED
SAGE LEAVES

½ TEASPOON DRIED
THYME LEAVES

5 CLOVES, GROUND

Combine all the ingredients in a large jar.

Each day, take 1 teaspoon in hot water.

Sparkling Elderflower

A non-alcoholic champagne or kombucha alternative! I learned a version of this recipe from Pat Collins when I took her natural first-aid kit course. We made all-natural remedies from plants and oils. It was amazing! I bought her book of recipes, tried this floral delight, and was smitten. She uses sugar; I prefer honey. Perhaps you don't care for any sweetener at all! Elderflower is another all-round healing plant: good for flus, colds and sinus issues. In this form, it's somewhat healing but primarily revitalising and invigorating. For a special occasion, serve with interesting ice cubes: prepare snippets of fresh mild herbs such as mint or lemon myrtle or perhaps fine pieces of citrus peel. Place delicately and artistically into your ice cube tray, fill with water, allow to freeze and then enjoy in your drink.

4.5 LITRES WATER
(1.2 GALLONS)

2 CUPS HONEY

1 LEMON

2 TABLESPOONS APPLE
CIDER VINEGAR

4 ELDERFLOWER
HEADS IN FULL BLOOM

STERILISED BOTTLES
THAT CAN BE FIRMLY
SEALED

Bring the water to a boil. Pour into a large glass container, stir in the honey then allow to cool.

Juice the lemon and chop the skin into pieces. Add, along with the apple cider vinegar and elderflowers.

Allow to stand for 4 days, stirring daily.

Filter, pour into bottles and seal carefully. Allow several centimetres for expansion.

Stand in a cool spot for 1–2 weeks in summer or 4 weeks in winter. If keeping beyond this timeframe, release some of the gas occasionally.

Smoothies: blend like a boss

Hands down, smoothies are the best thing to happen to breakfast since sliced bread. Blend seasonal fruit with ice or freeze the fruit then blend with water, coconut water or plant milk and enjoy. If you love chocolate, try blending a frozen banana with a tablespoon or two of cacao nibs, a teaspoon of maple syrup and a dusting of cinnamon. If you have a trusted sans-plastic source, add blueberries. Hey presto: breakfast is served. Even the most medicinal health powders or tinctures will taste good with this combo.

Looking to introduce turmeric to your morning? Blend together ½ cup frozen mango, ½ cup frozen pineapple, a teaspoon of grated ginger, ½ teaspoon of turmeric, a hint of pepper and a teaspoon each of chia and flaxseeds.

The challenge is to drink smoothies out of *glass* when you buy them. Smoothie tumblers were the hardest single-use plastic item for me to replace. Rarely will a cafe make you a smoothie 'for here' in a tall glass. Business owners hate the washing-up hassles. Better to quickly serve the next customer, keep 'em moving, and the dollars coming in. After having the full conversation with the staff about the negatives of plastic to-go cups and politely asking what it would take to offer jars 'for here', I'd look around for a suitable container. Usually there'd be a clean bowl. I'd ask them to serve my smoothie in this and enjoy it with a spoon. That's how smoothie bowls started for me.

A moment on single-use cups and bioplastics. Years ago, I stopped using paper cups when I learned they're lined with plastic to prevent leakage. What about the new biodegradable cups incorporating bioplastics – material made from plants yet chemically altered to resemble and act like plastics? Because they look like plastic, people get confused as to how to dispose of them.

In landfill, as bioplastics break down they emit methane, a greenhouse gas more potent than CO_2. The compost bin isn't correct, either. Commercial compost facilities that can break down bioplastics and return the by-products to organic matter are extremely rare. Waste management operations that separate bioplastics out from food scraps are too expensive for all but a very few local councils. Recycling is just as disappointing. Bioplastic cups are nonrecyclable, so if tossed in the recycling bin they actually contaminate this waste stream. It then requires time and money to filter out misplaced bioplastics.

There's a lot to unpack about this. First of all, it's a damn shame that every district, town, city, state and country has different recycling rules. An overarching national policy would make a lot of sense. However, recycling has been set up purely as a private business. We pay local councils for recycling bins. The council contracts a private company to come round and empty our bins into their truck. Unless the driver decides the material is contaminated – and takes the entire truckload straight to landfill – they drive the waste to the material recovery facility and dump it into a pile, ready to be scooped onto a conveyor belt for sorting.

Materials like metals, glass, paper and plastics are separated and sold to buyers on the global waste market. However, most countries have raised their standards for the materials they'll buy: contaminated materials are rejected.

There are small things we can do that make a huge difference. Help provide the recycling industry with cleaner materials to work with or our 'recycling' will keep ending up as landfill. Or just use less packaged stuff and have less in your bins! And maybe research our local material recovery facilities to find out what is recyclable.

And this is what we need: systemic change. Fewer disposable to go items and more reusables, refillables and repurposable items. This whole movement is about self-sufficiency and reclaiming our sovereignty. We should no longer rely on outsiders to recycle our waste. We must be autonomous and responsible for what we use and the waste our consumption creates.

Depressed? Don't be! Be a part of the solution and make yourself a smoothie bowl. Blend 1 frozen banana, 1 tablespoon tahini, 1 tablespoon flaxseeds, 1 teaspoon maple syrup, 1 teaspoon ground cinnamon, 1 cup ice, ½ cup nut milk, 1 teaspoon vanilla extract. Top with sliced fruit, toasted nuts, coconut flakes or granola.

3

BODY CARE

Recipe list

Reconnecting with your body

Our bodies are to be honoured. Worshipped. More nature. More love. More intention. We were made to move, made to get out in nature and connect. A crucial part of keeping this beautiful relationship going is looking after our skin: protecting and nurturing this giant organ encasing our blood and bones.

When I was young, I thrashed my skin. Throughout summer I'd be in the sunshine all day, lathered up with coconut oil and would rarely wash my face. During my college years, I caked on the black eyeliner and bronzer and took my clear complexion for granted.

Now that I'm in my thirties, I treat my skin with sacred rituals. I cannot avoid the sun, as I surf and sail and hike and swim, but I do try to avoid peak sun hours, I wear lots of layers and smear on my homemade sunscreen religiously. I have little glass jars and glass bottles that satisfy my need to pamper myself with myriad potions and romantic floral concoctions.

BEAUTY: MY PHILOSOPHY

In college, I was a philosophy major and I became fascinated with aesthetics, the branch of philosophy concerned with nature and appreciation of beauty. We puzzled over questions such as how to define what is beautiful. How can we agree on what is beautiful when what's soothing to one person may be jarring to the next? Are there universal beauty truths or is it decided individually, apart from some basic agreements within each society on what is beautiful?

Ultimately, I concluded that the more we're connected to our own sense of self, the more genuine we are in our interpretation of what's around us and our sense of what constitutes beauty. That's why I continually come back to practices that help me tune in to my essential self — like meditation, introspection, time spent in nature, yoga to settle the mind, breathing to connect to spirit.

I believe that our culture has intentionally numbed our sense of individuality, thereby numbing our ability to trust ourselves. As a consequence, we humans are easily influenced and quick to accept whatever we're told to think. Eerily, we've been convinced to focus our attention on media channels that tell us to buy things in order to be more attractive and successful. We're sold an unrealistic and highly unattainable concept of beauty. Not only does it perpetuate our dissatisfaction but it inspires us to consume more in the pursuit of beauty — or fill the void within ourselves.

The more I connect with my uniqueness, the less influenced I am by outsiders or swayed by majority opinion. I trust myself more.

As we cultivate our relationship with our true selves and with nature, we gradually realise that true beauty comes from confidence, from authenticity, from being empowered and connected to our sense of self.

As well as taking care of the planet, we need to take care of our bodies, our faces, our skin. I clean the beaches, I tend the garden, I pamper my flowers and succulents. So, too, I pamper my skin and, when I want to feel fancy, treat myself to wearing make-up. Without getting caught up trying to look like someone else or sacrificing my own unique nature.

Let's take a healthy approach to beauty and the rituals that make us feel loved up and looked after. We, too, are part of nature, so let's honour ourselves with the same attention with which we tend our gardens or pamper our babies or treat our most precious items.

NOT THE REGULATIONS YOU PROBABLY ASSUME

Generally, the USA is extremely lax about regulating cosmetics and beauty products. There's no requirement in US law for cosmetic products and ingredients, except for colour additives, to be approved by the Food and Drug Administration before they go on the market.

The make-up industry has been mostly self-regulated for more than a century. While governments in Canada and the European Union have banned upward of 1300 ingredients from use in cosmetics, the USA has only banned 11! It's left to consumers to fend for themselves when it comes to vetting product safety. In Australia, there's no agency dedicated to regulating the cosmetics industry. For instance, anyone can set up as a cosmetics manufacturer: you don't need a licence, and the Good Manufacturing Practice (GMP) isn't a mandatory accreditation. You don't have to submit your cosmetic products to any government agency for safety assessments or approval before putting them on the market. There aren't any specific government-mandated guidelines on testing cosmetics for safety and stability or lists for what the label must include.

Have trust issues yet? You should. But don't worry because with the recipes in this book I've got you covered. It's easy to make everything you need using simple, cheap and clean ingredients.

TOXINS

Sadly, many commercial products, even those labelled 'natural', contain preservatives and harmful additives. You won't notice immediately, but these build up over time. And when you start to feel unwell, you probably won't even question these everyday items that we tend to take for granted. If you don't recognise a listed ingredient, think twice about whether you want to absorb it into your bloodstream. Do you really know what the ingredient will do to your body? Do you trust the manufacturer? I invite you to do your own research on what you choose to avoid. Maybe start by looking into parabens, phthalates and 'fragrance'.

I realised that all those chemicals are hard for my body to process. My body cannot get nutrients from the sparkles added to my toothpaste that make it look cool on my toothbrush. My body is actually having to sort out all of those acids and synthetic fragrances in my face products and dump them through my lymphatic system. I am causing my body to work overtime for a short-term vanity. The more ingredients I read on the labels of common products found at the supermarkets, the more chemicals I added to my list to research. I got to the point where my list of toxins to research was longer than the natural herbs and plants to learn about. Most of what I discovered empowered me to ditch the store-bought altogether and get back to the mixing table.

Our bodies are already subjected to chemicals from the world around us — from air pollution, dyes or fillers in foods we eat at restaurants, cleaning chemicals in public spaces or the fresh paint in our workplaces or schools. Our bodies are taking in paint fumes through the lungs or harsh compounds through the skin, and then they have to get rid of those chemicals by metabolising them. The more chemicals we subject ourselves to, the more work our bodies do to fight and keep themselves clean. This leads to stress, breakdown and, ultimately, disease.

Ingredients in face scrubs, hair products, sunscreens and more have been linked to everything from hormonal disruptions to cancer, and what's worse is that when applied to the skin or hair, they go directly into your bloodstream. While there are certainly lots of studies with different perspectives on this topic, everyone can agree that using more natural products or — better yet, making your own — is the safest bet for you and the environment.

The best advice I can give is to minimise your exposure to chemicals as much as possible. I recommend making your own body-care products because you appreciate them more, save money, and can experiment to find the right combinations that work for you!

Over the past few years, I have felt like a literal flower blossoming in the sunshine. Nourished by rich revelations as I experimented with natural ingredients, I saw results from my hair to my skin to my teeth that were never achieved back when I was spending a fortune on products galore. My bath cupboards were filling with little glass jars full of oils and powders and little metal spoons and wooden brushes. Even just touching these items gave me joy. Now, whenever I have to touch plastic, I cringe.

BE EXPERIMENTAL

Depending on your skin type, climate and essential youness, some approaches and combinations of ingredients will suit you better than others. To start with, make small amounts of these recipes to see what works for you and enjoy the alchemical experimentation process.

The rule I follow is, 'If you'd eat it, you can put it on your skin.' This is far from limiting. There are millions of magical plants with an affinity for healing or revitalising the skin. All synthetic products are based on the properties of plants. It's also why the same wholesome ingredients crop up in so many recipes for different purposes. This is the beauty of connecting back to nature for our self-care routine. If it nourishes the hair, it probably nourishes the skin and can be used in masks and scrubs and mixed with oils.

Take raw, natural honey for example. It's primarily a food but it's extremely potent for healing wounds and lovely for the face as well, for instance in a mask with coconut oil. And oats are gentle and nourishing for the skin as they help to balance pH. If you're wary of oils or feel a break-out coming on, a gentle way to wash your face is with some rolled oats from your pantry. Pour a small amount into your palm. With the fingers of your other hand, add some warm tap water and blend into a paste, then gently massage onto your face. Rinse with warm water. It's all pretty much food! Enjoy the experiment and be open to your own discoveries. Rather than use expensive chemicals, come back to what's accessible in your garden and available in your pantry.

Not only does this approach save me hundreds of dollars every year, but when I use fresh ingredients, I know they're active. Purchased products can sit around for long periods at various stages of the supply chain before we get them home. By then, many of the ingredients we bought the product for are no longer active.

I find I'm much more consistent with using my homemade products because I know they won't keep forever, so there's no point in saving them for special occasions.

> *Tip: Use sanitised jars only! Think of it like storing food. It must be ultra clean or else it won't keep. Keep fingers and water out of them. Anything mixed with water needs to be stored in the fridge (the only exception seems to be vinegar, because it's a natural preservative) and anything involving fresh fruit and vegetables or dairy needs to be stored in the fridge and used within a couple of days.*
>
> ---

COCONUT OIL FOR EVERYTHING!

Most of us have probably gone through an epic coconut phase where it was dripping from our heads to our toes. Now, after a few years of sharing recipes, I realise this oil is not a miracle for everyone! It makes some people nauseous and clogs other folks' pores. I do my best to offer alternatives in this book of tips; however, this is all a result of my personal experimentation — which is the inspiration and intention for this section: be your own alchemist.

This is a guide. This is a little book of kitchen witchcraft where you can devise your own brews to suit your skin and hair. Let my recipes inspire you to make things, but do not stop there! Keep adding things to your cauldron until you find the magic. This book of spells is only your beginning.

> *Tip: Don't get water into your coconut oil (or any oils or honey): the oxygen in the water will cause the fat to ferment. To ensure these products last for as long as possible, only ever put clean spoons or fingers into your jars.*

A PLASTIC-FREE BATHROOM CABINET

The list of how to clean and care for our bodies with natural ingredients is endless. We can experiment and whip up various concoctions to soothe and nourish ourselves until the earth ices over. There are, however, a few more items I would like to recommend in your bath routine to avoid plastics.

MY FAVOURITE METAL BATH ACCESSORIES

* Safety razor — this is a stainless-steel razor with changeable razor blades. Each blade can last around three months. The razor can look ultra-intimidating at first, but as long as you go slow, you will get used to it.
* Tweezers — for splinters and unwanted eyebrow hairs.
* Nail clipper — you get it.
* Mini scissors — trim your nails and shape your eyebrows.

* Soap tray – as you substitute plastic bottles of shampoo and soap with solids, you'll need to place the soaps on little trays to help them dry out between uses.
* Tongue scraper – a small thin metal stick in the shape of a V that you gently drag along your tongue to scrape away plaque.

MY FAVE WOODEN BATH ACCESSORIES

Plastic will crack, stain and never break down. I use natural materials for my bath products and I find I treasure them that much more.

* Nail brush – look for bamboo with natural bristles.
* Bamboo toothbrush – there are tons on the market now. Try to find biodegradable bristles! Repurpose old toothbrushes into cleaning tools.
* Hairbrush – go for wooden brushes with wooden pins or else try a wooden or metal comb.

MY FAVE CERAMIC BATH ACCESSORY

* Neti pot – this is for a fabulous Ayurvedic practice of flushing the nasal cavity with warm salt water. (Best to do this in the morning.)

THE TRUSTY BAR OF ALL-PURPOSE SOAP

With this one item you can wash your hands, body and hair, plus you can use it to clean surfaces and fabrics. Wrap it in paper and use as a laundry stain stick or grate it, pop in a spray bottle and mix with water to make all-purpose cleaner.

I like to find a local soap maker – someone who makes organic natural soaps – and support their trade.

Bars of soap also make great gifts! Especially to friends or family who might want to transition away from household chemicals or plastic packaging but may not think of such an obvious plastic-free item. Find a paper-wrapped bar soap, place it in a seashell or on a cute plate from an op shop (thrift store).

Period accessories: going with the flow

Supermarket aisles are stocked with disposable pads made from bleached, fragranced plastic full of harmful phalates that take centuries to break down. Tampons are also bleached, fragranced and blended with plastic. Most tampons sold are made of rayon or a blend of rayon and cotton. Rayon is a synthetic fibre made from chemically processing wood pulp, which yields a highly toxic by-product called dioxin. Dioxin is a persistent and dangerous environmental pollutant.

I shudder to think that for the first years of my womanhood I was putting these bleached plastic 'sanitary' products inside of me or onto my most sensitive skin. The skin around the vaginal area is highly vascular (full of veins and other blood vessels), so is more permeable. Luckily, many more products are popping up to make us menstruators more comfortable.

It's important to discuss our periods and help break down the stigma and taboo around this beautiful natural rhythm half the world cycles through monthly for most of their lives. Half the population of the planet is a *lot* of people. We have to get all of these bleeders onto sustainable products because we're already seeing used pads and tampons piling up as hazardous plastic pollution and causing health risks. The more we talk about our periods, the more we normalise them. The more accessible all of these products will be.

Here are three innovative products that have absolutely changed my life. Don't let your flow hold you back. Get your equipment sorted.

MOON CUP

A medical-grade silicone reusable cup that you fold in half and slide up inside when menstruating. It will open once inserted and capture the blood. The shape of the cup creates a little seal, which prevents any leaks. Then every couple of hours, you dump the blood, clean the cup and repeat. Carry it in your bag in a small organic cotton pouch. Between cycles, soak the cup in hot water, then scrub with salt or bicarb soda and apple cider vinegar. Soak again. Store clean and dry.

REUSABLE CLOTH PADS

These wrap around your undies like plastic disposable pads, but instead of sticky glue, they use snaps to stay in place. It's far better for your sensitive skin to contact organic natural fabrics than the chemical-rich materials used in plastic pads. Soak in cold water after each use. Handwash with natural soap. Use salt to lift stains or bicarb for odour.

Many incredible humans are making these and selling them online. Look out for them at your local market. Best yet, make your own!

REUSABLE PERIOD UNDIES

These little padded undies changed my life! The monthly flow has certainly wrecked some of my favourite undies and I've also had my fair share of awkward moments being unprepared. When I wear these, my brain isn't constantly allocating 100% of focus to whether or not blood is leaking onto someone's beautiful white couch or through the G-string I wore forgetting the flow was coming. I can just be present.

Google some period undies for sale in your area or find a review page on my blog iquitplastics.com

Wash like your cloth pads: natural soap, handwash, line dry.

I carry all of these goodies in a little linen pouch during the bleeding phase of my cycle, so in times of need I can grab the required moon cycle stash and get on with living. In the bag is a little tin of bicarb soda for deodorising and cleaning while on the go, and a repurposed brown paper bag. If the pads and undies get saturated, I try to give them a big soak or rinse in cool water as soon as possible and hang to dry. If this isn't possible, I pour bicarb on the crotch, fold them up and put them into the paper bag, to be dealt with later. You can also harvest a plastic bag from a friend. Give it a great clean and repurpose it for your period undies.

Mouth care

Maintenance of the mouth is so important! The true goal of our dental routine is to prevent built-up plaque or neglected food from causing tooth decay. The actual paste does less work than the floss and toothbrush. If you want healthy teeth, brush more frequently and religiously floss. The paste is mostly a marketing ploy to sell you yet another product all dressed up in sparkly packaging with green stripes down the minty goop. If you can get used to a different sort of morning routine and let go of your attachment to the toothpaste you grew up squeezing from plastic tubes, you can make a real impact over the course of your life with reduced plastic packaging.

Toothpaste tubes don't get recycled. They're too small and have too many mixed materials jammed together: the plastic exterior, the aluminium interior, who knows what between. And it's all contaminated with sticky, gooey toothpaste. But, of course, our trash doesn't go 'away'.

Some of these discarded tubes end up in landfills in places like Indonesia, where waste pickers sort through these giant piles extracting anything that might have value. People in these places will separate out the plastic lids, shred the tube material — then use rerouted river water to clean the shred — and piece out any metal or plastic flakes to try and sell.

Meanwhile, the local water sources and rivers have turned to white minty sludge. No fish live there anymore, and the people have to pump the ground for their water.

Regular floss is plastic. And also typically coated in toxins: most floss gets coated with perfluorinated compounds (a chemical found in Teflon and linked to many serious diseases) to make the floss glide better. By now you should be used to me bursting the 'normal routine' bubble. It pays to adopt a sceptical attitude towards any product being manufactured by a large corporation and sold at a chain store. Question everything. Even this book!

> *Tip: In Australia, over 30 million toothbrushes are consumed every year. I find a lot of plastic toothbrushes on beach cleans and even when free diving in the ocean. Use a bamboo toothbrush. Many still have synthetic bristles, but at least the handles will compost in your backyard.*
>
> ———

Fortunately, there are a number of compostable and vegan floss products on the market these days. At all costs, avoid the single-use plastic floss picks! Spread the word: anything disposable is irresponsible, and these single-use plastics are heinously bad for the environment.

I also incorporate into my routine the ancient Indian hygiene practices of metal tongue scraping and oil pulling. Tongue scraping is believed to clear toxins and bacteria from the tongue, preventing bad breath, removing undigested food particles from the tongue, promoting overall oral and digestive health and gently stimulating the internal organs.

Oil pulling is an ancient Ayurvedic oral detoxification technique. Swish

1 tablespoon of oil (coconut, sesame or olive oil) in your mouth for 10–20 minutes and then spit it out. (Don't do this down the sink or you risk getting unruly build-up in your pipes!) This reduces the amount of harmful bacteria in the mouth. Bacteria create plaque or a thin biofilm on your teeth. This is normal, but if it builds up, it can cause bad breath, gum inflammation, gingivitis and cavities. Do this *before* brushing.

Toothpaste

This is a simple paste — not a thick cream with a long list of complicated-sounding ingredients — that will help clean your teeth! I'm obligated to advise you to consult your dentist before changing your dental-care routine. Please do your own research on this, but I'm a bit of a toothpaste sceptic. My approach is to brush frequently, floss regularly and use a few oils and rinses in the routine. Cleaning up the diet and limiting sugar will also help keep your teeth in good condition.

> *Note: Coconut oil is antibacterial, antimicrobial and antifungal. If you live in a cool climate, use more of this. In warmer climates, this toothpaste may become liquid. The solution is either to store it in the fridge or add more of the powders in the recipe to thicken the mixture. You may wish to keep a small teaspoon or wooden popsicle stick with your toothpaste to scoop a small amount of the mix onto your toothbrush. If you use a bamboo toothbrush, scooping with the wooden head will eventually cause the wood to rot. Try to keep any dipping to just the bristles.*

1 TABLESPOON
COCONUT OIL

½ TABLESPOON
ACTIVATED BENTONITE
CLAY OR NATURAL
KAOLIN CLAY (USE
A WOODEN SPOON
TO KEEP THE CLAY
CHARGED UP AND
ACTIVATED)

½ TABLESPOON SALT

½ TABLESPOON
BICARBONATE OF
SODA

1 SMALL GLASS JAR
WITH METAL LID

Pour the ingredients into the glass jar, then stir with a wooden spoon until thoroughly mixed.

VARIATIONS

Peppermint: add 1–2 drops peppermint oil, otherwise the toothpaste tastes salty and slightly weird!
Antibacterial: add ½ teaspoon activated charcoal powder. This doesn't whiten teeth but, because of its porous nature, it can draw out toxins and bacteria from the mouth.
For sensitive teeth and gums: replace the bicarb with more clay.

Note: Because it's polycationic (has more than one positive charge), bentonite clay can absorb negative-charge toxins, such as pesticides or heavy metals. It attracts and soaks up poisons on its exterior wall and then slowly draws them into the centre of the clay, where it is held in a sort of repository. This makes it handy in the mouth for toothpaste. Clay is also a gentle abrasive with a mild pH. It works well on the skin, too, healing skin lesions and drawing out impurities, so we use it in our skin masks. Sun lotions containing bentonite mineral are better than commercially available sun lotion at absorbing the highest level of UV light, so into the suncream it goes. It's even used to wash and soften hair! If using activated clay, scoop it out with a wooden spoon so that it can maintain its charge.

Travel Toothpowder

For travelling, or if coconut oil ain't your thing, here is a delightful blend of all of the herbs with an affinity for teeth. These work well in combination or alone, so if you don't have all the ingredients, don't worry. Gather the herbs from the garden and crunch them and rub them on your teeth.

Tip: Rub sage leaves on your teeth. Not only are they brilliant for cleaning but legend has it that they help whiten teeth!

Note: All of my little bath products are in small jars. When travelling, you want to wrap them in socks or arrange them to prevent them from shattering in your checked baggage and oozing minty fresh coconut oil throughout your belongings. And only pack jars with tested tight-sealing lids! But you don't need to be wary of oil spills – or additional weight in your luggage – with this toothpowder. I keep a stash with my travel gear in case I go on a last-minute adventure, so I always have tooth-cleaning options. Especially to avoid using the plastic hotel toiletries.

1 TABLESPOON DRIED MINT

1 TABLESPOON DRIED SAGE

1 TEASPOON DRIED THYME

1 TABLESPOON SEA SALT (SALT IS THE ORIGINAL TOOTH CLEANER! USE IT SOLO WHEN IN A PINCH!)

1 TABLESPOON BICARBONATE OF SODA (BAKING SODA): A MILD ABRASIVE (LESS ABRASIVE THAN COMMERCIAL TOOTHPASTES) THAT DISLODGES PLAQUE ON TEETH, BREAKS DOWN STAIN-CAUSING MOLECULES AND NEUTRALISES PH.

1 TABLESPOON BENTONITE CLAY

1 SMALL TIN OR TRAVELLING CONTAINER

If your herbs are fresh, make sure they're dry by leaving them in the sun or baking them with the salt until crispy.

Then, with a mortar and pestle, grind them to a powder.

Pour into a jar, then add the bicarb and clay.

Stir the ingredients together with a wooden spoon (metal deactivates the clay) or shake to mix.

For use, simply wet your toothbrush and dip the bristles into the powder for a light coating. Brush away.

Mermaid Mouthwash

I invented this easy-peasy and effective mouthwash when I was in remote Western Australia after my Whale Shark Mermaid Retreat, staying with Captain Bill and a bunch of other international gals. Being in such a remote part of the country with little access to bulk ingredients and very far from any healthy shops, I was pushed to experiment. Fortunately, the gals had excellent essential-oil stashes, and this minty-fresh mouthwash was born. The best thing that ever happened to my plastic-free health routine, it gives my mouth the most delicious fresh feeling after I brush and floss. Don't swallow these oils; spit them out!

---

1 DROP TEA-TREE OIL

3 DROPS PEPPERMINT OIL

FILTERED WATER

1 SMALL GLASS BOTTLE WITH METAL LID (SMALL JUICE OR KOMBUCHA BOTTLE IS PERFECT)

Fill the bottle with filtered water, then add the essential oils. Done!

Remember that the oils will separate from the water when sitting on your shelf, so always give this a good shake before using and definitely spit this out. Do not swallow.

> *Tip: Try blending in 1 tablespoon of fresh aloe vera gel (see instructions, page 169) into your mouthwash! Aloe is incredibly effective at reducing dental plaque. It kills plaque-producing bacteria in the mouth.*

Note: Essential oils often come packaged in little glass (yay!) bottles with plastic lids (boo!). Buy the largest you can order/ find. Split it among friends. When you finish the bottle, send the container back to the manufacturer asking for a refill. Suggest metal packaging or setting up a refill system. You can also make your own herb-infused oil. This is not as strong as distilled essential oil, but it is gentler on the planet.
(See page 197 for infusions.)

Glowing skin, clean body

Skin is a beautifully complex organ. It protects us from infection; millions of nerve endings allow us the sensations of touch; it continuously renews itself; it moisturises itself with oils; it excretes wastes; it's strong, flexible and sensitive; and it hosts heaps of friendly micro-organisms. Making our own products from natural ingredients ensures that we're in harmony with nature and, more importantly, with our own nature.

Most skincare products marketed to us contain chemicals and artificial ingredients that could have a short-term benefit and likely negative long-term impact. The skin absorbs chemicals into the bloodstream and the chemicals can lodge in your cells.

Avoid putting harsh, artificial ingredients onto your skin, near your eyes, onto your beautiful face! Make a point of reading the labels. Not only are many of the ingredients a worry, but the plastic container is also likely to leach chemicals into your toner or anti-aging cream.

I couldn't believe this when I first heard, yet wasn't surprised: many anti-wrinkle remedies don't heal and regenerate your skin, but instead fill the cracks with microplastics to make it appear as if the wrinkles have gone. These chemicals can actually contribute to premature aging or spike your oestrogen, leading to weight gain or depression. This is definitely not your intention when you invest in beauty products.

Healthy skin begins with healthy insides. If you're having any skin issues, look at your diet and habits. And remember to hydrate. An easy way to moisturise from the inside out is to simply drink water. Hydration can mean the difference between dry, wrinkled skin and smooth, plump, healthy skin.

Incorporating steam into your routine helps increase circulation to the face, opens the pores and absorbs moisture. Add flowers and herbs to your steam for an extra lush experience. Rose, calendula and chamomile all reduce inflammation and tone and calm the skin, thanks to their natural astringent and antihistamine properties. Use rosemary or green tea for deep-pore clarifying and anti-aging.

Drink a generous amount of water, then cleanse your face. Now bring to the boil a saucepan of water, add the herbs of your choice and leave to boil for a few minutes. Pour into a large bowl that's wrapped in a towel to set on your lap or on a table where you can sit and hold your face above it. Make sure it's secure and won't fall onto you. Burning yourself is not part of this skin treatment; be very careful. Drape a towel over the bowl of tea plus your head and shoulders so the steam is contained. Keep your face 20–30 centimetres (8–12 inches) away from the tea and steam for around 5 minutes. Remove the towel and sit down if the heat feels too intense.

Apply a face mask, exfoliate or rinse with warm water. Pat the face with a wet warm towel and apply face oil.

Oils: simple, effective skincare

'What do you do for face wash?' 'What moisturiser do you use?' 'What should I use for lotion?'

My answer is the same for all of the above: oils. A long time ago, following the principle that if you'd eat something, it was probably safe to put it on your skin, I experimented with oil. The versatility and effectiveness of oils impressed me. Turns out the best solution is the simplest.

Surprisingly, oil dissolves oil, which is why it works as a cleanser. Unlike store-bought foaming cleansers, this approach doesn't strip skin of its natural oils and bacteria barriers. Oils used for cleansing (most common choices are olive oil and coconut oil) may also have healing properties, important nutrients or other skin-boosting benefits.

When it comes to moisturising, the oil needs to be paired with water. The oil locks in the water that's already absorbed by your skin. So, if you saturate your skin by taking a shower, you'll lock in a lot of moisture by immediately rubbing oil all over your body.

CAUTION: For a few people, oil can cause an allergic reaction, irritation or clogged pores. If you have skin issues, consult your dermatologist before trying this approach to skincare. Even if you don't have issues, apply a small amount of the oils on a patch of your skin for a couple of days to see how your skin reacts before launching into the oil skincare routine.

THE OIL SKINCARE ROUTINE FOR YOUR FACE
It may take 3–4 weeks of regular oil cleansing to achieve balanced skin. Resist the urge to use harsh soaps or facial cleansers during this time, as it will disrupt the adjustment! Some people find their skin gets worse initially, which can be a detox reaction as impurities are pulled from the skin.

1. Massage your dry face. Pour ½ to 1 teaspoon of oil into the palm of your hand and rub your hands together. Using a circular motion, gently

massage the oil into your face for a few minutes. This softens hardened plugs of sebum lodged in pores, breaks up blackheads, releases dirt and removes make-up. It also helps to release tension and improve circulation, thus firming up skin.

2. Steam. Run a soft washcloth under hot water, wring it out and cover your face to open your pores and hydrate your skin. Repeat as much as feels good. This will create steam to open the pores and help remove any impurities in the skin. Leave the washcloth on for about a minute or until it cools. Remove eye make-up last.

3. Clean. Gently wipe your face with the hot washcloth. Try not to drag your skin – it's delicate at this stage. It should feel soft and clean.

4. Tone. Spritz your face with your chosen toner. This restores balance to the skin's pH.

5. Oil. While your skin is damp, lock in that moisture by massaging in a drop or two of your favourite facial oil (see below).

CHOOSING THE RIGHT OILS

Opt for pure, unrefined cold-pressed oil from nuts or seeds. These contain beneficial antioxidants, fatty acids and other nutrients. Olive oil is the most popular choice, with coconut oil second. Never use vegetable, canola, shortening or corn oil! Avoid oils stored in plastic.

The following is a basic list. I've been able to procure all of these in glass with metal lids.

* Oily or acne-prone skin: sunflower, apricot, grapeseed, sesame, rosehip seed
* Normal skin: olive, sunflower, almond, apricot, sesame, rose hip, jojoba
* Dry skin: avocado, olive, macadamia nut, almond
* Aging skin: sunflower + rosehip seed (great source of vitamin C), macadamia, coconut

Try these with friends, so that you don't waste money on a whole bottle. But hey, if there's one you don't like on your skin, you can always use it in the kitchen! Woohoo!

Rosewater Toner

I pair oil cleansing with water-based toners. Rosewater is cooling, calming and hydrating; chamomile is soothing and anti-inflammatory; and green tea is balancing for oily or acne-prone skin types. Apple cider vinegar is also an option for post-cleansing toning of the skin. We don't need all of the expensive chemical creams; we just need to practise making a tiny bit more time for ourselves. All of these water-based toners can also be used for face cleansing and rinsing the hair.

5–10 ORGANIC, FRAGRANT ROSE HEADS (USE PESTICIDE-FREE ROSE PETALS SO YOUR ROSEWATER ISN'T FULL OF TOXINS)

1 LITRE OF WATER OR ENOUGH TO BARELY COVER THE FLOWERS IN A LARGE SAUCEPAN

Gently rinse the rose heads with warm water to remove any dirt.

Place the roses in a large saucepan and add enough water to just cover (no more or you'll dilute your rosewater). On low heat, bring to a simmer and cover.

Allow to simmer for 20–30 minutes or until the petals have lost their colour or are a pale pink.

Allow to cool. Strain the mixture to separate the petals from the water.

Compost the petals and pour the rosewater into dark amber glass. This helps it keep longer, as rosewater has a limited shelf life (1 week out of the fridge, 3–4 weeks in the fridge). To use, tip a teaspoon into your palm and apply to your face.

Tip: You can use this as a hair rinse, natural perfume, mood-enhancing spray – and more.

Aloe Face-glow Moisturiser

The Egyptians called aloe vera the 'plant of immortality'. It promotes skin cell regeneration, which is why it's used for cuts and burns. Aloe vera gel contains anti-aging antioxidants such as beta carotene and vitamins C and E. It also has gibberellin, which acts as a growth hormone stimulating the growth of new cells, supporting quick healing without scarring. In a study of 30 women over the age of 45 who applied the gel of aloe vera to their faces, it was found that collagen production and skin elasticity increased over a 90-day period! I say, why not get this green miracle goop onto our faces on a regular basis!

This is a powerful oil-free moisturising option that grows abundantly and is ready to use straight from the ground. Aloe vera gel is light, absorbs quickly and offers a delightful cooling sensation for red, inflamed or normal skin. It moisturises without giving the skin a greasy feel, thus is ideal for oily skin. For those who use mineral-based make-up, aloe vera gel moisturises and prevents skin drying. For men, aloe gel can be applied after shaving to heal small cuts and irritation.

Some people find aloe irritates and causes redness, so patch-test on your skin. If you experience irritation, wash with cool water.

1 LEAF OF ALOE VERA

1 TEASPOON WATER

GLASS JAR TO STORE

Cut open a leaf of aloe. Slice off the spiky edges, then slice off the green skin on both sides, leaving a long, slimy translucent slab of aloe.

Blend this with water and strain through a nut milk bag into a bowl to prevent your moisturiser from being chunky. Use the remaining goop for a face or hair mask while you finish preparing your Aloe Face Glow Moisturiser.

Store in the fridge and apply to your skin after cleansing and toning. Suitable for both day- and night-time use. This is nice for summer but it may be too cooling in winter.

Note: Aloe vera is extremely easy to grow, no matter where you live in the world. If you're in a warm climate, plant outdoors. If you're in a cool climate, your aloe vera plant can thrive indoors if you position it in a sunshine-drenched part of the house. Plant your aloe vera at any time of the year, with sand and rocks mixed in with the soil to ensure good drainage. Water it regularly to show your appreciation and nurture it as you hope it will nurture your face! Then gratefully slice its leaves as you need.

Face or Body Cream

Although I prefer oils to cream, many people prefer creams. Here's a basic recipe that can get you started on your own cream creations.

---

3 TABLESPOONS OIL
(CAN USE
PLANT-INFUSED OIL,
SEE PAGE 197)

3 TEASPOONS
BEESWAX

3 TABLESPOONS TEA

CLEAN GLASS JAR

Melt the oil and wax in a double-boiler (see instructions below).

Slowly pour the hot tea into the bowl of oil and wax while stirring vigorously with a fork or whisk.

Pour the cream into a clean jar and allow to cool before use. If the cream sweats, just pour off excess liquid.

Tip: Quite a few of my recipes call for a double-boiler (where one saucepan sits directly and snugly over another saucepan of boiling water) because the ingredients – such as beeswax – need to be stirred steadily over indirect heat. There's no need to buy a double-boiler: fill the bottom saucepan ¼ full with water and bring to the boil. Reduce the heat to a simmer, place the ingredients in a heatproof bowl and perch the bowl on the saucepan, making sure it sits nicely, without wobbling, and doesn't contact the boiling water directly. Stir the ingredients constantly as they melt.

Tea-tree Oil Acne Spot Treatment

Pimples are never invited to the face party, yet sometimes they rudely show up and hang out for ages. Tea-tree essential oil works absolute wonders for those pesky pimps, plus it's harvested from the abundant native Australian melaleuca trees that grow locally. Love! The tea-tree oil works because it dries out the oil deposit that is the zit; we want to avoid drying out your skin too much, as that could trigger your body to overproduce its own oils and make acne worse. If you have witch hazel, you can blend 20 drops of witch hazel with a drop of tea tree for a gentler pimple treatment.

TEA-TREE OIL

Put your finger over the bottle opening and turn it upside down. Dab the small amount of oil directly on the pimple. If this is too strong for your skin, try diluting with water. Leave it.

Apply light face oil to the rest of the skin and pat near but not on the pimple.

VARIATION

Combine 1 teaspoon of bicarbonate of soda (baking soda) with 1 teaspoon of warm water. Apply the paste to the acne. After 2 minutes, wash with warm water.

Invigorating Coffee Butter Bars

This delicious oiling bar smells like brown sugar and lavishes your skin like an ordinary soap bar never could. I started making these as an experiment. I could only find caustic lye packaged in plastic, so making my own soap was out. When I tried wax and oil, this little bundle of joy popped out. It's so worth the extra effort! Remember that beeswax requires high heat to clean up, so be sure to give the bowl or saucepan you use a good wipe with hot water.

¼ CUP CACAO
BUTTER

¼ CUP COFFEE-
INFUSED COCONUT
OIL

1 TABLESPOON
BEESWAX

½ TEASPOON CACAO
POWDER

½ TEASPOON
GROUND CINNAMON

Using a double-boiler on low heat (see instructions, page 170), melt the cacao butter, coconut oil and beeswax together.

Remove from heat and stir in the cacao powder.

Pour melted butter into a mould or mini muffin tin.

Let mixture cool until hardened.

Pop out the bars and store in a tin or jar in the fridge.

Should last 6 months to 1 year.

VARIATION

To make a Citrus Rose Butter Bar, follow the recipe above but infuse your coconut oil with rose petals and replace the cacao and cinnamon with 1 teaspoon lemon zest or orange rind.

Use when still wet in the shower. As mentioned earlier, you want to oil up after your shower to help lock the moisture from the shower into your skin. Be aware it might drip on the floor. If that happens, clean up immediately so no one slips!

Exfoliation: replenishing the surface

For healthy glowing skin, get into the routine of exfoliating once or twice per week. Gently scrubbing the skin in circular motions removes dead skin cells and promotes the growth of healthy new ones. This also helps improve circulation and invigorates and tightens the skin, giving it a firmer appearance, evening out skin tone and improving texture. The longer dead skin cells hang out on the surface of the skin, the harder they become. With age, this layer thickens, making the skin look dry and flaky. Exfoliation gives new skin time to shine and helps reduce wrinkles.

Remember, I'm not a skincare specialist; I'm a mermaid alchemist. Do your own experimenting and never try anything that *intuitively* doesn't sound or feel right for you. If a scrub is too abrasive, it can leave tiny scratches on your skin or break blood vessels. Spot test first to ensure it feels nice, especially on your face.

LOOFAH
The *best* exfoliator can be grown in your garden: loofahs are plants that grow on a vine and resemble a large cucumber. You let them rot on the vine, then the exterior peels away, leaving the porous inside. After it dries, it hardens to become the loofah we know and love for our shower time!

BODY SCRUBS FROM YOUR PANTRY
No need to drop cash at the spa when your kitchen has plenty of grainy goods! It's easy to repurpose coffee grounds, use plants or cheap ingredients like sugar for scrubs, provided you don't mind a bit of mess in the shower. Be careful you don't clog up your plumbing by combining these with coconut oil too frequently.

Orange: eat the fruit, then use the white inside of the peel to wipe your face, neck and décolletage. The gentle white pith acts as a soft exfoliator and the citric acid removes that top layer of skin, allowing the vitamin C to be absorbed. But watch out for the citric acid: this can be strong for sun-sensitive skin: use only at night, especially if you're in the sun a lot.

Other softer exfoliants suitable for the face include oats, nut meal (e.g. the discarded almonds from your milk), ground flowers and herbs. Mix in a small bowl with water, warm tea, honey or oils to make a gentle paste. Essential oils can add another dimension.

Sugar is a natural humectant, meaning it draws moisture from the environment into the skin. It's an effective exfoliant plus it has natural glycol acid that restores a healthy fresh glow to skin. This is good for sun-damaged or aging skin. This is great for a scrub, but can be too rough for the face. To avoid microtears in the skin, aim for the smallest granules, like brown sugar, if you can find it in bulk. If you can only find white, use sugar for body scrubs and opt for oats on the face.

Australian Natives Sugar Scrub: purchase Kakadu plum powder from the Palngun Wurnangat Association, a women's organisation based in Wadeye, Northern Territory. You'll be supporting the largest Aboriginal community in Australia. Add a small amount to a mixture of macadamia oil and sugar. Kakadu plum powder has 100 times more collagen-promoting vitamin C than an orange.

Coffee grounds are packed with antioxidants that help protect skin from free radical damage that causes aging. They can be good for cellulite and stretchmarks, too. Sometimes the caffeine is absorbed through the skin and you may feel a slight buzz! If you're sensitive to caffeine, maybe keep this one for the morning. Coffee grounds can feel harsh on delicate skin, so if that's you, sticking to oatmeal may be a better choice.

Salt has antiseptic qualities, so on the skin it may help kill bacteria and reduce inflammation, along with any itching and pain associated with bacteria-related skin disease. Mixing salt with oil is best, as on its own it can strip the oils from the skin. With its relatively large and coarse granules, salt is good for exfoliating the body or rougher patches of skin.

Lip Scrub

When our lips are cracking and dry it can be a sign we need to drink more water. It's also a nice practice to give your kissers a gentle scrub once a week to keep the lip skin supple. Apparently, lips don't have sebaceous glands to keep them moisturised whereas our skin secretes sebum to keep it hydrated and nourished. We have to clear away the dead skin before we can moisturise our lips. Scrub regularly and apply balm.

½ TEASPOON FINE
GRAIN SUGAR

½ TEASPOON OLIVE
OIL OR COCONUT
OIL

Mix together in your palm.

Apply to your lips.

Rinse with warm water.

Apply Lip Balm (see page 203).

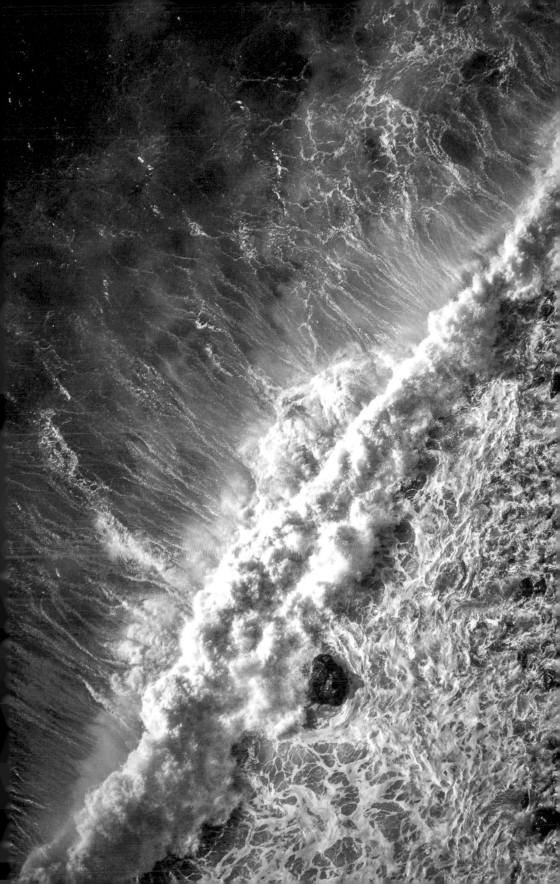

Best Deodorant Ever

While it makes us whiffy, sweat has an awesome function — cooling
our bodies. This is one of my favourite recipes because it's incredibly
simple and incredibly effective and has been approved by really active
people, from ballerinas to builders. The bicarb deodorises, the arrowroot
powder absorbs moisture, and the coconut oil binds together the powders
plus is antimicrobial, antifungal and antibacterial. Be sure to apply your
deodorant *after* you apply oil to your face, otherwise the slightly abrasive
bicarb from the deodorant will be lingering on your fingertips!

Note: For sensitive skin, replace bicarb soda with a natural
clay powder such as kaolin clay or bentonite clay.

———————

1 TABLESPOON
BICARBONATE OF
SODA (BAKING
SODA)

2 TABLESPOONS
ARROWROOT
POWDER OR
CORNFLOUR

3 TABLESPOONS
COCONUT OIL

OPTIONAL

10 DRIED ROSE
PETALS FOR
AESTHETIC APPEAL
AND GENTLE AROMA

2 DROPS ESSENTIAL
OIL OF CHOICE
(AVOID IF YOU
HAVE SENSITIVE
UNDERARMS)

SMALL SHALLOW
GLASS JAR WITH
METAL LID

Using a chopstick or the handle of a spoon, mix the ingredients thoroughly. It isn't necessary to melt the coconut oil first, but this can make for easier mixing. Transfer mixture to glass jar.

For use, simply dip your fingers in or rub across the top until a light layer forms on your fingertips, then spread to other fingertips and use opposite hand to apply to opposite underarm.

This mixture may liquify in warmer climates. If it does, make sure the seal is tight, flip the jar upside down, and put into the fridge until the liquid solidifies.

When you unscrew the lid, a tiny lip of deodorant should extend just beyond the edge of the jar; this allows you to roll the paste across your underarms like conventional deodorant.

Store in a cool dark place.

> *Tip: If your deodorant is too runny, the quick fix is to add more arrowroot.*

Zoe's Warm-weather Pit Paste

I spend a few weeks a year in a biologically diverse wonderland in Western Australia, where I take mermaids and mermen swimming with whale sharks and other incredible marine creatures. This place is warm all year round and my regular deodorant recipe isn't effective. But when my beautiful marine biologist friend Zoe started adding beeswax to her deodorant, which made the product solid, it worked like a charm. Thanks for sharing your recipe, Zoe!

½ CUP COCONUT
OIL

3 TABLESPOONS
NATIVE BEESWAX
FROM A LOCAL
BEEKEEPER

½ CUP ARROWROOT
OR CORNFLOUR

2 TABLESPOONS
SODIUM
BICARBONATE

Melt coconut oil and beeswax (cacao butter is the vegan option) then add dry ingredients, stir until smooth then pour into a jar and allow to set.

If you want to add essential oils for scent, wait until the mixture has started to cool otherwise the heat will evaporate the scent and you'll need to add more.

Tip: If you run out of your homemade stash of deodorant or find yourself in a moist-underarm situation, apply either apple cider vinegar or lemon juice to a clean underarm. (Improve your digestion and you won't smell!)

Luscious Tinted Sunscreen

Every year 14,000 tonnes of sunscreen enters our oceans. Over 65% of that contains a chemical of high toxicity concern, oxybenzone. According to research, one drop of oxybenzone in an Olympic-sized pool of seawater creates a toxic environment for coral. Oxybenzone is also now recognised as a human endocrine disruptor. Zinc oxide, provided it is non-nano and uncoated, is a natural mineral that provides an effective and far safer barrier to protect against UV rays. It reflects the sun's rays rather than absorbing them. The particles in non-nano-particle zinc oxide are sufficiently large that they don't penetrate the skin and enter the bloodstream. You don't want the skin-penetrating nano-particle zinc oxide. Most suppliers will know the difference and help you find the correct product.

Unfortunately, zinc oxide comes packaged in plastic. Personally, I haven't found a supplier where I can avoid the mineral being packaged in plastic. So I bought the largest bag I could find and despite having sunscreen-making workshops, make-party gatherings with friends, and plain giving it away, I have barely made a dent in the powder! Once it is eventually empty, I will rinse out this thick plastic bag and use it in my travels when I have to pack wet clothes or I'm worried about one of my bottles leaking. Once the bag is no longer useful, I'll take it to a Redcycle bin at either Coles or Woolworths (Australian readers only).

¾ CUP COCONUT
OIL

¼ CUP BEESWAX

¼ CUP ALMOND OIL
(OR OLIVE OIL OR
HEMP OIL)

1 TABLESPOON
GRAPESEED OIL OR
JOJOBA OIL

¼ CUP SHEA BUTTER
OR CACAO BUTTER

½ CUP ZINC OXIDE
(NON-NANO AND
UNCOATED)

2 TABLESPOONS
CACAO POWDER

1 TEASPOON
GROUND
CARDAMOM

1 TABLESPOON
CARROT SEED
ESSENTIAL OIL
(NOT SUITABLE FOR
PREGNANT WOMEN)

Bring the water in a double-boiler to the boil (see instructions, page 170). Put all oils except for the carrot oil, beeswax and butters in the top of the double-boiler.

Stir constantly over low–medium heat until the butter and wax have melted.

Add in the zinc, cacao and cardamom and stir until the mixture is well combined.

Pour into a shallow glass jar. Then add the carrot seed oil and stir.

When ready to use, spread onto your skin gently and thoroughly. Reapply every few hours.

Store your jar in a cool dark place.

> Note: Cacao butter melts at a high temperature, making it ideal for the baking-hot temperatures of peak summer. Shea butter is a great option for a winter sunscreen.

Hand Sanitiser

While you can use essential oil or a combination of oils for this hand sanitiser, I prefer tea-tree because you can get it locally in bulk in Australia. Do your best with what you have locally.

¼ CUP FRESH ALOE VERA GEL (SEE INSTRUCTIONS ON PAGE 169)

1 CUP DISTILLED WATER

1 TABLESPOON FRESH LEMON JUICE

20 DROPS TOTAL OF ANY OF THE FOLLOWING ESSENTIAL OILS: CINNAMON, CLOVE, TEA-TREE, ROSEMARY, EUCALYPTUS, LEMON, ORANGE, GRAPEFRUIT

Pour the aloe vera gel into a dispenser.

Add the lemon juice and essential oil(s).

Put the lid on and shake.

Bye-bye Bug Balm

I grew up in Minnesota, a progressive state in the middle of the USA's northern border. It's where the Great Lakes and surrounding boundary waters of Canada spill into America. Known as the 'land of 10,000 lakes', Minnesota is the original home of the Lakers basketball team — I have lots of state pride! It was a beautiful place to grow up and I have fond memories of summers spent at camps, on lakes or at cabins with family and friends.

But I digress: bodies of water mean mosquitos! Back in the day, we'd shower our entire bodies in horrible toxic spray in order to withstand outdoor activities. I cringe thinking of my little skin cells shrivelling up as I doused them in harsh chemicals every hour. Especially as I now realise this was entirely unnecessary. All it takes is a thin layer of this ointment to keep the bugs away.

10 TEASPOONS OILS
(SEE NOTE BELOW)

1 TEASPOON
BEESWAX

SMALL TIN OR
GLASS JAR (IF YOU
CAN, WARM THE
CONTAINER)

½ TEASPOON LEMON
JUICE

2 DROPS
EUCALYPTUS
ESSENTIAL OIL

3 DROPS TEA-TREE
ESSENTIAL OIL

2 DROPS LAVENDER
ESSENTIAL OIL
(OPTIONAL)

Melt the oils and beeswax in a double-boiler (see instructions, page 164), then remove from the heat.

Once the wax is totally melted, slowly drizzle in the lemon juice with one hand and continuously whisk the mix with the other hand to help it emulsify.

Using an oven mitt, pour this into the warmed container.

Quickly add your essential oils, put the lid on and shake vigorously for 5–10 minutes or until you feel the mix form from liquid into a thicker cream. Allow to sit and solidify.

Note: Any combination of your favourite oils will do.
Here's what I like:
4 teaspoons grapeseed oil
4 teaspoons almond oil
2 teaspoons coconut oil

Sugar Leg Wax

Most razors on the market are disposable plastic ones. I use a stainless-steel safety razor and I have also had laser hair removal. This is my personal choice based on my desire for hairless legs; you do you! If you're up for waxing your own legs, here's an entirely compostable — though I must admit, time-consuming — way to remove that luscious body hair of yours.

---

1 CUP SUGAR

¼ CUP LEMON JUICE

¼ CUP WATER

POPSICLE STICK

PAPER BAG (RIPPED INTO STRIPS) OR A CLOTH CUT INTO STRIPS (WASH IN HOT WATER AND REUSE)

Whisk the sugar, lemon juice and water in a small saucepan.

Heat the mixture over low heat and wait 10–15 minutes until it turns amber brown. Stir only 2–3 times.

Pour the sticky syrup into a plate or bowl. Allow it to cool a bit, then use a popsicle stick to spread onto your skin. Be especially careful; don't burn yourself!

Cover with a paper bag strip, then quickly rip off!

You may need to heat the mixture up a few more times if it cools too much to spread on your leg. Also, be sure to compost the waste when you're finished!

Make-up

This has been one of the hardest categories to find and create plastic-free alternatives for. Maybe it's partly because I'm not a frequent make-up wearer. Having said that, I do like to cover up the sunburn on occasion or smoky up the baby blues for a fancy dinner out. I totally believe in self-care and self-love and the importance of enjoying how you look. I have friends who wear a face of make-up every day that lasts from 7am, when they leave the house, through a full day of work, maybe socialising afterwards, and then home — 12 or more hours later — with the make-up completely intact. That's a hard act to follow.

What motivates me to hold my nerve in this arena is my awareness of the myriad chemical additives in those products, the fact that were likely tested on animals and stuffed full of preservatives to kill any living bacteria that could reduce its shelf life value. It's a bit scary to consider that we smear this stuff directly on our eyes and mouth.

I've developed this selection of facial sprucer-uppers to make us feel Cleopatra-glam without all of the little plastic tubes and plastic wands, and of course all of the laboratory-concocted chemical cocktails that largely go unregulated.

There are some great plastic-free, all-natural make-up makers emerging, which is exciting. Up until now, I've survived on simple food-based powders and making small batches of eye make-up just for the night or the weekend.

This make-up works, and it lasts for a good amount of time! Having tried a tonne of ingredient combinations, from beeswax to coconut oil, once again, I can confidently state that the simplest ingredients worked best! These make-up recipes have two or three ingredients that likely already live in your pantry! Loving the simple life even applies in the beauty department.

Face Powder and Bronzer

There's a certain amount of trial and error involved in finding the right combinations for homemade make-up: what you add to the base will depend on your skin tone. Use arrowroot powder for lighter skin and turmeric powder and/or ground paprika for warmer skin. I add cardamom to my basic face powder, but you'll want to go for a really finely ground powder. For my bronzer, I add cacao powder.

Once you get the blend of edible, face-safe powders right, you'll be able to top them up as required from your pantry! My face powder is made from pretty much the same ingredients as my morning tonic! That's a pretty epic endorsement for the health factor, y'all.

BASE

¼ TEASPOON CACAO POWDER

⅛ TEASPOON GROUND CINNAMON

OPTIONAL

⅛ TEASPOON GROUND CARDAMOM

⅛ TEASPOON ARROWROOT POWDER

⅛ TEASPOON TURMERIC POWDER

⅛ TEASPOON GROUND PAPRIKA

Using a teaspoon, you might start off making your face powder with some cacao and cinnamon as the base ingredients, then applying it to your skin with your powder brush to see how it looks on you.

If too dark, add some cardamom or arrowroot.

If the colour isn't warm enough, add a pinch of turmeric or paprika.

Continue to blend and experiment. Be sure to write down each addition and in what quantity.

Store in a repurposed container and apply to skin over the top of your homemade skin-tinted sun cream (see page 182).

Shimmer Face Powder

The purpose of the zinc oxide is to incorporate sun protection. It also helps with the coverage of the foundation and contributes a matte finish. While I feel safe using zinc oxide on my skin (only the non-nano and uncoated variety, mind you), you may not. If so, replace the zinc oxide with arrowroot powder and replace the mica with ground cinnamon. Bear in mind that you'll sacrifice the staying power of the finished product.

---

2 TABLESPOONS ZINC OXIDE (NON-NANO AND UNCOATED) FOR SPF

1 TEASPOON GOLD MICA DUST

½ - 1 TEASPOON OF NATURAL WHITE OR GREY CLAY POWDER

1 TEASPOON FINELY GROUND CACAO POWDER

½ TEASPOON BRONZE MICA POWDER FOR DESIRED COLOUR

Mix all the ingredients and tweak the quantities of coloured mica powders, natural clays (bentonite is great) and cacao powder until you achieve the colour that's right for your complexion. Start slowly and add those ingredients as needed, testing on your inner-arm as you go to find your shade.

Store in a small glass jar with a lid.

Tip: If you have oily skin, add 1 teaspoon of arrowroot powder.

Foundation Cream

By adapting Shimmer Face Powder you can create a foundation that protects against the sun and also has a bit of shine. You may want to apply the powder-mixing principles used in this section (e.g. in Face Powder and Bronzer, page 192) to get the right skin-tone match.

SHIMMER FACE POWDER (SEE PAGE 193)

2 TEASPOONS JOJOBA OIL

1 TEASPOON COCONUT OIL

½ TEASPOON MELTED CACAO BUTTER

½ TEASPOON ALOE VERA GEL (SEE INSTRUCTIONS, PAGE 169)

¼ TEASPOON WITCH HAZEL

Mix up your Shimmer Face Powder and put aside. In a small bowl, whip together jojoba oil, coconut oil and melted cacao butter with a fork until uniform. Then whip in the aloe and witch-hazel.

While cream ingredients are still liquid, slowly add in 2–3 teaspoons of Shimmer Face Powder. Stir until evenly mixed. Test in small amounts on the back of your hand to ensure desired consistency and blend into skin with the pad of the ring finger to match to skin tone.

Use colour-blending techniques to achieve desired tone: if too dark add cardamom or arrowroot; if too light, add a pinch of turmeric or paprika etc.

The cream may be thick if you are in a cooler climate, or liquid if you are in a warmer climate. Add more oils if you desire a thinner foundation, but compensate with adding equal powder.

Store in a small glass jar with a metal lid.

Natural Blush

To make this more coral-coloured, add $\frac{1}{16}$ teaspoon turmeric. For a mauve tint, instead add $\frac{1}{16}$ teaspoon of cacao powder.

¼ TEASPOON
ARROWROOT POWDER
OR, FOR ADDED SPF,
REPLACE WITH ZINC
OXIDE (NON-NANO
AND UNCOATED)

¼ TEASPOON
PINK POWDERS,
ACCORDING TO
COLOUR PREFERENCE

Blend the ingredients together in a bowl and adjust the ratio to achieve your desired colour.

Store in an old make-up container or an old compact.

> *Note: You can find naturally occurring pink powder in red clay (the lighter this is in colour, the less arrowroot powder you will need), beetroot powder (purchase from bulk food store), dried hibiscus flowers (use only if you can grind organic flowers to a very fine powder) or pitaya powder (purchase from bulk food store).*

> *Tip: If you currently own store-bought make-up, save all of those little containers and bottles. Soak them in hot vinegar water to loosen up any leftover residue, then air-dry.*

Flower water: floral magic in a bottle

For an excellent alternative to expensive essential oils, flower water, or floral water, is a winner. Put simply, it's water with a floral aroma made by soaking blossoms in water – in much the same way you make an infusion or a tea – or by enhancing water with essential oils.

Flower water has all kinds of uses. You can drink it as potent medicinal tea, inhale the steam and fragrance, rinse your hair with it, spritz your skin with it, apply it as a facial toner or spray it on your body to lift your energy. You can sub these into any bath or beauty recipe that uses water – all of our sprays, creams, facial toners, hair rinses, shampoos or conditioners – to give the mix an indulgent, sweet fragrance.

You could even incorporate these flower waters in your cooking and baking! Flavour your raw cakes with floral water nut milks or use flower water in your chia puddings.

Our bodies assimilate teas and flower-water infusions with ease: the common denominator is water. Despite our engagement with our flesh and structure, and the solid feeling of our day-to-day experience, we're made mostly of water. The same goes for our planet.

The process of making flower water can be a beautiful nature-connection ritual. You always want to use organic flowers that haven't been sprayed with chemicals or pesticides. What was put on the flower or into the soil will end up in your flower water. Buying a bouquet from your local supermarket won't work. Also, being water-based, flower waters are prone to contamination by mould and bacteria. If that worries you, the solution is to carefully sterilise your containers beforehand. Plus you could consider adding preservatives like vodka or witch hazel. Keep your flower water refrigerated and toss it back in the garden if the aroma changes or the water gets cloudy.

THREE TYPES OF FLOWER WATER

Sunshine Flower Water – Add flower petals (e.g. the petals of 6 large roses, grown without pesticides) to a 1-litre jar of filtered water. Allow to sit in the sunshine for two weeks, shake every day if you can. The longer you let them steep the better the smell – but the more patience required! Strain out the petals then add more fresh ones and repeat the sunshine infusion. Do this as often as you like until desired aroma is achieved.

Witches' Brew Flower Water – Add rose petals and water to a double-boiler (see instructions, page 170). Slowly simmer and stir in your intentions until the colour has left the petals. (This method is quicker and less labour-intensive than the process of steam distillation, but the end product may not be as strong.)

Healing Tea Flower Water – This is the same process as making tea! We're simply infusing water with the plant material. Place the materials of your choice in a jar, pour boiling water on them, cover the jar with a tight-fitting lid and allow to sit for 5 hours. Use 1–2 teaspoons chopped fresh herbs, flowers or aromatic dried seeds per 1 cup boiling water.

Steeping times:
flowers 1–3 minutes
leaves 2–4 minutes
seeds 4–10 minutes.

To make Brightening Flower Facial Tonic, bring 2 cups of water to the boil, remove from the heat, then add 1 handful of fresh, fragrant rose petals, 2 tablespoons lavender buds and 1 handful of fresh mint leaves. Cover and allow to sit for 30 minutes. Strain the mixture and discard the plant material, then add 1 handful more of rose petals. Allow to sit in the sun for 30 minutes more then pour in ½ cup vodka as a preservative. It's up to you whether you leave in the rose petals or strain the liquid and discard. Store in a repurposed spray bottle (in which case, to use, you can directly spray a fine mist onto your skin) or a small glass bottle (pour a little into your palm and then pat your face with clean wet hands).

Mascara

Be warned: making this can be messy. Beeswax sticks to everything and then promptly hardens. Charcoal powder goes everywhere. Put newspaper down and clean up constantly as you work. If you can, keep a set of utensils — a bowl, spoon and saucepan — that are exclusively for preparing beeswax recipes, so you don't ruin your fave kitchenware. Or be diligent about washing with hot water straightaway and wiping clean with newspaper.

I often add freshly blended aloe vera gel (see page 169) as well, although this can make the mixture a bit clumpy, so I recommend you stir and swirl the black goop and then remove any clumps of aloe vera to keep your mascara smooth and homogeneous.

You can remove this mascara from your eyes with olive oil or coconut oil.

Note: Depending on your climate, you may need to adjust the ratio of coconut oil and beeswax. If you're in a hot climate, the coconut oil may melt and smear onto your eyelids, so you may need to add a bit more cacao butter or beeswax. If you're in a cold climate, the beeswax may harden completely and be impossible to spread on your lashes. Try running your container under hot water to soften the mascara up before application. Alternatively, reduce the beeswax.

½ TEASPOON
COCONUT OIL

¼ TEASPOON CACAO
BUTTER

¼ TEASPOON BEESWAX
(IF YOU LIVE IN A
HOT CLIMATE, USE ½
TEASPOON)

¼ TEASPOON
ACTIVATED CHARCOAL
POWDER

⅛ TEASPOON
TRIPHALA (OPTIONAL:
THIS IS AN AYURVEDIC
POWDER FOR EYES)

⅛ TEASPOON
BENTONITE CLAY

⅛ TEASPOON
ARROWROOT POWDER

½ TEASPOON FRESH
ALOE VERA GEL (SEE
INSTRUCTIONS, PAGE
169)

CLEAN MASCARA
CONTAINER OR SMALL
TIN

CLEAN, REPURPOSED
MASCARA WAND (TO
APPLY)

Melt the coconut oil, butter and beeswax in a double-boiler (see instructions, page 170).

Stir in the powders with a toothpick until smooth.

Scoop into a small tin or glass jar.

Stir in the aloe vera gel.

Eyeliner

This works for full eyes or a subtle wing, depending on if you want to be fabulous or just accentuate your natural look. This recipe also doubles as mascara. Keeping it simple wins again.

BLACK

¼ TEASPOON ACTIVATED CHARCOAL POWDER

¼ TEASPOON ARROWROOT POWDER

½ TEASPOON ALOE VERA GEL (SEE INSTRUCTIONS, PAGE 169)

BROWN

1/20 TEASPOON ACTIVATED CHARCOAL POWDER (SO VERY LITTLE IS NEEDED!)

⅛ TEASPOON ARROWROOT POWDER

¼ TEASPOONS CACAO POWDER

½ TEASPOON ALOE VERA GEL (SEE INSTRUCTIONS, PAGE 169)

Put powders into a small container.

Add just enough aloe vera gel to make a thick paste (a toothpick is perfect to mix it with).

Use an eyeliner brush to apply your eyeliner. If you don't have this, get creative! Please be safety conscious when experimenting with tools to apply your eyeliner. Avoid sharp objects near your eyeballs! You could check op shops for small brushes. I find that the fine-point dull needles used in various needlework crafts do the trick to dab the ink on the lid!

COLOUR COMBINATIONS

Brown: cacao powder, ground cinnamon
Tan: ground cardamom, cacao powder
Green: spirulina powder
Blue: blue algae extract
Red: beetroot
Pink: pitaya or acai powder

Tip: Mica powder comes in a range of colours and is useful for highlighting. Buy in bulk, e.g. online or from the bulk store. Ask suppliers to pack in paper bags or send them a jar to fill. If we as consumers express our desire for better packaging, the suppliers will eventually capitulate!

———

Note: Experiment with different textures. Start with just one or two drops of aloe vera gel and keep mixing more in until your eyeliner reaches the consistency you want.

———

Eye Make-up Remover

Either aloe vera gel or oil works fine for this. If you want a fancy separate product for make-up removal, here ya go!

½ TABLESPOON RAW HONEY, IDEALLY MANUKA

½ TABLESPOON ALOE VERA GEL (SEE INSTRUCTIONS, PAGE 169)

3 TABLESPOONS CALENDULA OIL

Pour all the ingredients into a very clean or sterile wide-mouthed jar or bottle, and shake to combine.

Test in a discreet spot to check for irritation.

Store in the fridge.

Orange Blossom Tinted Lip Balm

I'm all about getting as much turmeric in and around my body as possible, so why leave it out of my beauty routine? Here's another way I sneak it in!

½ TABLESPOON
BEESWAX

½ TABLESPOON
CACAO BUTTER

½ TABLESPOON
COCONUT OIL

½ TABLESPOON
ALMOND OIL

¼ TEASPOON CACAO
POWDER

⅛ TEASPOON
TURMERIC POWDER

Melt all the wax, butter and oils in a double-boiler (see instructions, page 170).

Stir with a toothpick until fully blended.

Add in the powder and stir again.

Pour into your lip balm container.

VARIATIONS

Naked Cacao Tinted Lip Balm: increase cacao powder to ½ teaspoon; omit turmeric powder.
Pink Rose Tinted Lip Balm: replace cacao powder and turmeric powder with ½ teaspoon beetroot powder. (I wouldn't recommend using fresh beetroot juice: it's too watery. Thinly slice beetroot, dry in the sun or oven, then grind to a powder. This will achieve a darker shade than bulk-bought beetroot powder, which tends to be quite pink. Adjust the quantity to obtain the desired shade.)

The intuitive art of self-love

It's so important to slow down and create some self-love time. Give yourself the gift of chilling. Invite over a pal or two to make some plastic-free delights. Make a big healthy dhal and drink tea together. Then put on the records, light the candles and try concocting a few of these recipes! Take photos and tag me @Plasticfreemermaid so I can see and live vicariously through your cruisey times!

A night to myself to drink tea, listen to podcasts or old soul records and experiment with new takes on a plastic-free product or two is a dreamy solo date. Once I have my ingredients out, I treat myself to a face and hair mask while I experiment.

Pamper yourself throughout your sustainable witchcraft session. Apply coconut oil to the ends of your hair for a conditioning mask. Wrap your hair up in a warm damp towel or just tie it back out of your face. Wash your face with warm water. Mix a detoxifying, anti-inflammatory bentonite clay mask (just mix warm water and clay; stir with a wooden spoon or stick because metal spoons deactivate the clay's magical powers). Keep on your face for 10–15 minutes or until hardened. Wash, allow skin to breathe for a few minutes. Then smooth with either olive oil or aloe vera gel.

Practise feeling into your body: you have all the answers within you. What does your skin need? Ask it: oil or aloe vera gel? Close your eyes and let your body tell you which it wants. The first word that's whispered or known is the one. This is your intuition guiding you back to you. Use this throughout your day. Coffee or tea? Yoga or run? Notice the ego trying to weigh in. Practise waiting for the intuition, the deep knowing to guide you on your highest path. In these little moments, we can practise so it's strong for important decisions.

One way to achieve the pampering of self-love and connecting to nature in a moment is a touch of floral oil, which can linger for hours on our skin; little wondrous whiffs can sweeten any day. The practice of concocting oils slows us down and helps us develop patience; both are so important for our beauty and self-love routine. We don't want to rush through this. We want to enjoy and take it all in.

FLOWER-INFUSED OIL

Stuff lavender leaves and flower buds into a jar or bottle and pour oil over. It should cover your botanicals with 2.5 centimetres (1 inch) oil to spare. Place the bottle in a warm spot but not in direct sunlight. Every day for 2–6 weeks, shake the bottle or flip it upside down. Pass through a sieve, press the flowers and then discard. If the scent isn't strong enough, gather more flowers and repeat. If you like, dry the lavender first to avoid fresh moisture from clouding the oil.

SOLID PERFUME WITH FLOWER-INFUSED OIL

The ancient Egyptians made solid perfume from beef fat boiled in sweet wine. I find blending 10 teaspoons of Flower-infused Oil (for a variation of the above recipe, try jasmine or rose) with 1 teaspoon melted beeswax in a double boiler (see instructions, page 170) achieves the same effect with more efficiency. Pour into a small jar or tin with a tight lid and dab on pulse points at wrists, inner elbows and neck.

SOLID PERFUME WITH ESSENTIAL OILS

I hesitate to advocate for using essential oils since most come in small glass bottles with black plastic lids. Black plastic doesn't get recycled in traditional recycling facilities as the optical sensor doesn't pick up the colour. If you can make your own or buy from a local source in your own container, opt for this regenerative solution. In a double-boiler melt together 3 teaspoons almond oil, 3 teaspoons grapeseed oil, 1 teaspoon beeswax and 3 drops rose essential oil. Pour into small clean jars and stir in the essential oils with a toothpick. It's important to get the cap on as quickly as you can to prevent the essential oils from evaporating. Allow the mixture to set. Apply to pulse points to release the perfume.

Hair

Some of us have more hair than we have face. Some of us are outdoors or in the ocean so much that the back-of-head tangle is borderline dreadlocks. Happily, for managing the mane, there are heaps of amazing shampoo and conditioning bars on the market.

Going natural not only reduces plastics but it limits our exposure to toxins.

Despite their attractive ads and billion-dollar fragrance blends, those glamorous shampoos are full of nasties that, if properly labelled, we'd never let near our heads and bodies on a daily basis. Maybe one bottle of that stuff won't affect us, but over time the chemical load will build up in the body.

Shampoos often contain silicones, which make our hair appear healthier when, in fact, they're coating and suffocating our strands. Even shampoos free of silicone are full of additives that haven't been tested for long-term impact and really aren't necessary to simply rid our hair from dirt and excess oils produced by the scalp. Since the birth of the #NoPoo trend, people have ditched shampoo altogether. Amazingly, they're not hiding away in shame: quite the opposite! They're whipping their luscious locks around with poo-free pride. Since switching to these simple haircare routines, my hair has grown into long, strong mermaid locks. It helped that I also ditched my heat-styling tools and embraced my natural waves.

I've experimented with different approaches to haircare and keep coming back to the same basic ingredients: bicarb and vinegar. This stuff works for literally everything. Give this a try, but know that all hair is different and we're in different climates, exposed to different pollutants and engaged in different activities. If after a few weeks these don't work for you, try shampoo bars. If you return to shampoo, try buying it in bulk.

Tip: In Indonesia, dandruff is treated with pineapple, and aloe vera gel is rubbed into the scalp to encourage hair growth.

Simple Shampoo

If the aim is to clean the hair, this one-ingredient shampoo does the job. I've found that I need shampoo far less now that I've forsaken the daily lather of my teen years. When I feel my hair is greasy, I just sprinkle through some bicarb soda and step into the shower. Occasionally, I switch things up by using bentonite clay and water. After washing your hair with the Simple Shampoo, follow with the Simple Conditioning Rinse (page 210): apple cider vinegar conditions like a dream.

---

2 TABLESPOONS BICARBONATE OF SODA (BAKING SODA)

2 CUPS WATER

Mix bicarb and water in an old spray bottle or shampoo bottle. Apply to crown of your head – where you set your crown, Queen! (Queen: fabulous embodiment of royalty; fitting for all genders.)

Massage into your scalp like normal shampoo. Rinse.

> Tip: The water in your shampoo bottle will go room temperature, which can feel chilly in comparison to hot shower water. If this bothers you, like it does me, make a fresh batch for each shower with 1 teaspoon of bicarb to a cup of warm water.
>
> ———

Bread Head Wash

I learned this from my Instagram community. So grateful for the platform to connect and learn from each other. Thank you for sharing what works for you! It seems counterintuitive to spoon flour into your hair. However, rye flour contains natural saponins and is full of vitamins, minerals, amino acids and even Omega 3 fatty acids. It has a pH of 5.0 so it won't disrupt the natural pH balance of your hair and skin (4.0–5.5). This is a super-gentle way to clean your hair. If the result is naturally soft, shiny, luscious locks, the method can be as weird as it wants!

---

2 TABLESPOONS
SIFTED RYE FLOUR
(DOUBLE FOR LONG
HAIR)

1 CUP WARM WATER

Sift the rye flour through a tea strainer to get any large flakes out.

Mix this with lukewarm water with a fork or small whisk until thoroughly combined.

Standing in your shower to avoid mess, put the flour in your hands and apply to your head. Brush it in. It won't foam. It won't smell like flowers. It will clean your hair.

Shower and rinse it out. If you don't get it all out, brush it again when it's dry and it will fall out.

Simple Conditioning Rinse

Apart from a nourishing mask every couple of weeks, all I use to condition my hair is this apple cider vinegar (ACV) rinse. I wouldn't have thought dumping acid water on your head would be good for you, but it works wonders. The vinegar seals the cuticle of the hair, making it less prone to breakage and improving lustre! If you dye your hair, this can help maintain the colour. This is so cheap and simple, you have to try it.

---

1 TABLESPOON APPLE CIDER VINEGAR (SEE RECIPE PAGE 222)

1 CUP WATER

1 SMALL GLASS BOTTLE

OPTIONAL

A FEW DROPS OF ESSENTIAL OIL (IF THE SMELL IS TOO HARSH)

TWO SPRIGS OF FRESH ROSEMARY (SUPPORTS HAIR GROWTH AND VOLUME)

FRESH CHAMOMILE (REPUTED TO LIGHTEN HAIR)

SAGE (REPUTED TO DARKEN HAIR)

Mix everything together in the bottle.

For use, shake the mixture, spray or pour approximately 3 tablespoons worth around the crown of the head (i.e., not directly on the top of the head but where a crown may rest on your head).

Allow to saturate the hair, then rinse out.

Store the main bottle under the sink. If desired, add a few sprigs of rosemary and allow to infuse.

Notes: Often the ACV gets blamed for the drying of hair, when it might be the bicarb soda from the Simple Shampoo. If it feels as if your hair is drying out, try massaging coconut oil into the ends at night.

———

Before each use, top up the jar with warm water to avoid a chilly shock. As the mixture runs out, add more ACV to maintain the ratio. It doesn't need to be very precise.

———

Coconut Conditioning Hair Mask

Washing with bicarb and rinsing with vinegar is cheap, easy and effective. It does necessitate that occasionally we treat our locks to something special, like a nourishing hair mask. I recommend this once or twice a month. For extra points, go to bed with your hair wrapped up in a towel. Having said that, if you have an important event, maybe hold off on the treatment as your hair will still be a little oily the next day. Alternatively, apply the mask only to the ends of your hair.

COCONUT OIL

Simply massage your hair with coconut oil from roots to tips. This will help strengthen hair and bring back moisture, which will bring back shine. Take care to massage your scalp with your fingers and allow yourself to enjoy this sensual act.

> *Tip: I tend to lather up my sundrenched hair with whatever in the kitchen looks moisturising. From avocado and olive oil to honey. Some intuition coupled with some traditional wisdom. My study of Ayurveda and my independent research of various cultural remedies has led me to discover blends such as rosemary warmed through olive oil or ½ avocado, ½ can coconut milk and 1 tablespoon coconut oil.*

Dry Shampoo

Back in high school, we used to hide the grease in our hair with baby powder. I went to an all-girls school, so we weren't prioritising glamour. I kept it up long after graduating, perhaps dusting my roots after a sweaty workout or if my ocean hair didn't get washed when it should have. When I quit plastics, the little plastic baby powder bottle got cut. I started hunting for a similar powder to keep my natural scalp oils at bay in emergencies.

---

1 TABLESPOON
BICARBONATE OF
SODA (BAKING SODA)
OR ARROWROOT
POWDER, OR BOTH
TOGETHER!

DARK HAIR
1 TABLESPOON CACAO
POWDER

OILY HAIR
1 TEASPOON CACAO
POWDER

½ TEASPOON
ARROWROOT

½ TEASPOON
BICARBONATE OF
SODA (BAKING SODA)

Dip fingertips or a make-up powder brush into the jar or bowl, and massage into scalp and hair roots to help absorb grease.

You can use this on an as-needed basis or keep a little jar handy – at the office, in your gym bag, etc. – and apply regularly.

> Note: If these don't work for you, try using bentonite clay. I know you'll have it in your pantry by now!
>
> ———

4

CLEANING

Recipe list

Detox your home

The last thing I want my home to be is a sterile environment that's teeming with toxic chemicals lingering from cleaning products.

Unfortunately, because most cleaning products aren't required to label ingredients, we have no idea what we're spraying on our table tops and counters. We blindly trust that since it was sold at a big-name store, it must be safe. This isn't true. Many corporations have patents on chemicals and combinations that bring about impressive results for the intended effect, but the health impacts aren't considered. It's only after tonnes of research and lawsuits that harmful chemicals are removed from shelves. It isn't an easy process, thus most chemicals — harmful or not — stay right there on the shelf hidden inside the plastic container with no identifying ingredients list to reveal the nasties within.

The kitchen is where we spend time preparing food. The bathroom is where we take warm showers that open our pores. Toxic fumes that linger from cleaning products won't keep to themselves.

Generally speaking, I'm risk taker. I swim with sharks and dedicate my time to saving the world. But risking my health would eliminate all the fun I like to have. So I'm pretty practical when it comes to avoiding chemicals that will cause me harm over my lifetime. Consequently, I've experimented and come up with recipes that work just as well.

As an aside, for a friendly vibe and to filter the air, get a heap of house plants. (Don't forget to open the windows as often as you can, too.)

CLEANING MATERIALS

A zero-waste cleaning routine relies on durable tools that can be washed and reused. The opposite is cheap synthetic sponges that flake, rip and get soggy. Go for cleaning materials that are non-toxic and natural and look for products so clean that they might even be edible. If that feels unreasonable, at the very least use cleaning products that won't toxify your home by leaving unhealthy residues that your loved ones then touch. Make the cleaners yourself, then you avoid filling up the garbage bin with empty, dirty containers and cloths that need to be hauled away to landfill. Right now, some of the most effective cleaning agents there are already live in your kitchen.

SPRAY BOTTLES, TUPPERWARE AND REUSABLES

I try to avoid buying any plastic at all, and while I use spray bottles in many of these recipes, I avoid buying new ones. Always. There are plenty of plastic bottles already out there in the world. We can collect these from neighbours or co-workers. In a similar vein, I also use Tupperware containers.

As with all my reusables — especially the things I carry with me constantly to avoid using disposable plastics — I value them, keep them clean and keep track of them. It's true that the more you love an item, the more you'll use it. If you don't really care about the cup or spoon, you will forget to bring it out or leave it somewhere. Saying, 'Oh, just this one time' whenever we use something packaged in plastic is a very slippery slope. Even when we put it into the recycling bin, that one-time disposable bottle has a hair-thin chance of being recycled into something of lesser value. Knowing that plastic takes somewhere around 1000 years to fully break down back to organic matter, not even one little lid or packet is tempting to me. I'd rather take five minutes to make a product at home. And most of the products I share with you here are literally that quick and easy to make.

MAKE LIGHT OF IT

When it comes to cleaning, the same basic ingredients do an epic job for most cleaning needs. That lends itself to good things like buying in bulk and experimentation with different combinations of the following ingredients to perform different cleaning tasks:

* bicarbonate of soda (baking soda)
* lemon
* vinegar
* bar soap
* eucalyptus or tea-tree essential oil

If I'm especially lucky and I have easy access to soapberries, then my cleaning game shames the store-bought toxins!

Seeing a pattern here? Plastic-free is simple, cheap and easy!

General cleaning

Our homes are our safe refuge. Caring for our space is important. The more natural products we use, the more we can trust and fully relax.

TIPS FOR SUCCESS

* Collect and save your plastic spray bottles. (Don't have any? Post on social media for friends to save their bottles for you.)
* All cloth goes to landfill: create one final purpose for old clothing by cutting it into rags. Tear up T-shirts and linens that are past their prime. Wash and reuse them. No need for paper towels, which leave little white streaks on your glass: use rags. When they wear out, compost them.
* Repurpose bra and swimsuit boob inserts for cleaning sponges!
* Give old toothbrushes a second life as scrubbers for intricate or hard-to-reach places.
* Make your own scrubber from the husk of a coconut or knit one from twine or rope.
* Grow or scavenge compostable brushware: from loofahs to coconut-husk brushes to rough sea sponges, there are many excellent scrubby brushes to be found in nature.
* Sweep with a wooden broom with natural bristles! Compost your dust.
* Cut an old cloth into long strips and tie onto a long stick for a homemade mop! Wash your floors with a few drops of eucalyptus oil in a large bucket of water. Avoid disposable wet floor wipes (or wipes of any kind!) They have plastic woven in, so they don't biodegrade and can cause serious blockages in sewer systems.

CLEANING SOLUTIONS FOR QUICK WINS

Here are some of my favourite quick-and-easy recipes. Cruise around the house holding a cloth in one hand and a container with any of these in the other. In a short time, you'll achieve sparkling cleanliness!

* Warm water and 1–2 drops eucalyptus oil.
* Grate a basic bar of all-purpose soap into a spray bottle, mix with water and shake.
* Neat vinegar. White vinegar is hard to find in bulk. I tend to buy apple cider vinegar in glass or make my own (page 222). The smell does tend to linger longer, which prompted me to develop Citrus Vinegar as an alternative (page 223).
* Tea Liquid Cleaner. Combine 1 cup of fresh tea from fresh or dried herbs with 2 tablespoons of borax or Washing Soda (page 231). This effectively cleans, deodorises and disinfects walls, fridges, tiles, china and crystal.
* Use coconut oil to remove carpet stains, for spots on upholstery or for removing chewing gum! Coconut oil can be purchased in bulk in reusable glass containers.

Apple Cider Vinegar

The process of making a vinegar or alcohol is to combine fruit and water and leave it to ferment. Bacteria will consume all the fruit's sugar and convert the water into acetic acid, or vinegar.

PEELS FROM 10 CLEAN
APPLES*

ENOUGH WATER TO
COVER THE PEELS

LARGE WIDE-
MOUTHED JAR

Collect apple cores and skins or peel and core a bunch and use the apple flesh for an apple pie or fruit salad. (*First, vigorously scrub the skins to make sure they're free of wax and pesticides.)

Place peels in the jar and add water. Cover and leave in a warm place to ferment.

Each day, stir to aerate. Remove the froth as it ferments.

Taste the liquid every few days. The taste of vinegar will gradually develop.

Once the liquid has developed a full vinegar taste, there's no more alcohol to ferment and it has stabilised. Strain into a jug and compost the peels. Pour into bottles.

Note: You can save a small amount of the vinegar in a jar as the 'mother' to make more vinegars. Feed her with peels and water sporadically until you have enough peels to begin the process again.

———

Citrus Vinegar

For an excellent window cleaner, add 3 tablespoons Citrus Vinegar to 1 litre water in a spray bottle. Use newspaper to polish. Store remaining liquid in a jar below the sink for general cleaning.

5–10 CITRUS PEELS

½–1 LITRE OF VINEGAR (WHITE IS PREFERRED IF YOU CAN FIND IT IN GLASS)

A NARROW JAR OR WIDE-MOUTHED BOTTLE

Put peel and vinegar into container and screw on the lid.

Leave to stand for 2 weeks in a cool dark cupboard.

Strain and put to work! Add to 1 litre warm water for soaking pots with burnt-on tough-to-remove grease.

Tip: Save the lemon wedges from your salad dressings or morning teas and the rinds from your morning tonic and pop them into a big jar. After a week, you should have enough to make your vinegar!

General Cleaning Spray

Remember to repurpose old spray bottles for these tasks. If you don't have any of your own, enlist help from friends or co-workers. Avoid using bottles that previously held products full of chemicals: plastic actually absorbs toxins, so bottles that held toxic chemical mixtures are now full of harmful nasties! This is another reason recycling is more complicated than originally thought.

---

2 TEASPOONS
TEA-TREE OIL

1 TEASPOON
WASHING SODA
(PAGE 231)

REPURPOSED SPRAY
BOTTLE FULL OF
WATER

Put tea-tree oil and washing soda in the old spray bottle.

Fill with water.

Shake before each use. Spray onto the dirty surface then wipe with a rag or newspaper (suitable for glass and metal surfaces).

The top three cleaning wonders

Check out what cleaning products you currently have under the sink and do some ingredient research. Once you're thoroughly freaked out, take a deep breath and check your pantry for the top three wonders of the natural world: lemons, vinegar and bicarbonate of soda (baking soda). I could clean my entire house and everything in it with just these.

Bicarb can do pretty much everything. I sprinkle it on dirty surfaces and scrub away. I use it for absorbing odours (place ¼ cup in an open container and leave it to work its magic), clearing drains (see Vinegar Drain Flush instructions below), shining silver (bring to a boil 1 litre of water, 1 tablespoon of bicarb, and one piece of aluminium foil, drop in your silverware and remove after 10 seconds with kitchen tongs), killing mould (combine with white vinegar in a repurposed spray bottle; spray onto the surface and wipe clean), and more.

Buy it in bulk in reusable containers. Keep a spice shaker full of bicarb soda handy to sprinkle on fresh spills. Store it under the sink ready to sprinkle on dishes for a cheap effective clean.

Lemon wedges will clean and shine your metal sink, oven and taps (just rub with the peels and compost the leftovers). Leave a paste of lemon juice and salt on rust marks then rinse off with water. Lemon also works wonders on germy surfaces like baths and toilets (sprinkle with salt and use a wedge of lemon to scrub).

Vinegar disinfects and softens fabrics in the wash (replace detergent with ½ cup white vinegar or your homemade vinegar: see pages 222 and 223), cleans vegetables, floors and toilets, clears odour, clears drains and works well when mixed with baking soda. Add a drop of essential oil for scent.

VINEGAR DRAIN FLUSH
Prevent blocked drains by pouring a kettle of boiling water down the drain weekly. This can be pond or ocean water if you're in a drought! The key

is ultra-hot water to de-glug any glugginess. If you need something with more power, drop ½ cup bicarb down your drain or toilet, followed by ½ cup vinegar. Leave it for 5 minutes, then flush with a kettle of hot water. For heavy clogging, repeat several times.

VINEGAR RINSE

Before you put away your newly purchased fresh fruits and veggies, give them a soak in a sink of fresh water with add a cup vinegar in it. You can also make a veggie spray (in a spray bottle that never held anything toxic). Give your veggies a spritz then scrub with a coarse brush to help remove the nasties. Rinse in water. This will clear any dirt and harmful sprays from their skins. If using the sink method, remove the produce and let the dishes have a turn.

Scum left on your freshly washed dishes could be salt lingering from the tap water or perhaps from the soap.

To help cut this residue, add a cup of vinegar to your rinse water. Be water-wise. Wash your dishes in soapy water in one sink and have a bowl or second sink for a quick dip and shake before leaving the dishes to drip-dry on a rack.

VINEGAR SPRAY

Often, surfaces that are cleaned with soaps feel like they have a thin film. Spray and wipe with diluted vinegar. (This is the same concoction we use to clean veggies! You don't need a million cleaners, just a can-do attitude to whip these up at home. Which is literally just a splash of vinegar in a bottle of water.) Add 1 tablespoon lemon juice to enhance the scent. Or if you have essential oils add a drop of lavender or tea tree.

VINEGAR WINDOW AND GLASS SPRAY

For shiny clean windows and mirrors, spray on a mixture of vinegar and water and rub dry and then polish with scrunched up newspaper.

Aromatic Smudge Sticks

Purify your air and cleanse any energetic funkiness by burning some lovely home-grown or locally grown herbs. Not much burning is needed to bring the delightful smells and vibrations of nature indoors.

SPRIGS OF ROSEMARY, SAGE, THYME, FENNEL LEAVES AND STALKS, LAVENDER, OR PINE

COTTON THREAD (OR TWINE)

Pick fresh healthy herbs. Holding their stems together, wrap them into little bundles with cotton thread (don't wrap with synthetic thread!) with a finger width spacing between each wrap.

Let them dry out on display; place them around your home as decoration. They're quite nice in the bathroom.

Once your smudge stick is dry, hold the end over a flame, then blow it out and let the embers burn. (Use matches or light from a stove; plastic lighters will be washing up on beaches for centuries and centuries long after you are dead and gone.)

Allow the thin trail of fragrant smoke to swirl and clear the air and lift the energy.

Kitchen

A considerable amount of plastics-related action happens in the kitchen, whether it's storing foodstuffs, preparing food or cleaning dishes and surfaces. People used to get along fine without plastic, so maybe ask an elder if you get stuck for ideas.

If you can buy castile soap in bulk, do so. It's a dependable, gentle natural soap that you can use on floors and kitchen surfaces; you can wash dishes with it, shampoo your dog, and use it for your hands, body and hair. The list goes on. If your local supplier packs it in plastic, however, maybe make your own!

With dishwash liquid, it's tough to match the consistency and sudsing ability of the soaps we can buy at the supermarket. But most of them are manufactured with synthetic thickeners. When we choose to live plastic-free we make adjustments; opting for the natural soap may take some getting used to. A homemade dish soap may settle or be quite thin, thus will squirt out fast. So be sure to let any legends who volunteer for dish duty know it's 'easy does it' on the soap squirting.

For effective dishwashing while using water sparingly, it's best to get all dishes free of food, dumping as much food waste into the compost bin (never your trash bin) as possible and then either washing them straightaway or at least soaking them in the sink right after use, so that food doesn't crust on. Plug the sink then wash all of the dishes. Rinse them in a separate sink to reduce water use. Let them dry in the rack or use a tea towel.

Washing Soda aka Dishwasher Powder

If necessity is the mother of invention, perhaps accident is the father. When I couldn't find washing soda for sale sans plastic, I discovered you can make sodium carbonate from sodium bicarbonate by baking it in your oven! Use this homemade washing soda as you would store-bought — in natural cleaning recipes, laundry soaps and more.

BICARBONATE OF
SODA (BAKING SODA)

BAKING TRAY

AIRTIGHT CONTAINER

Preheat the oven to 200°C (400°F).

Pour a 1.5-centimetre (½-inch) layer of bicarb onto the baking tray.

Bake for 1 hour, stirring once or twice partway through, or until the bicarb has changed in look and feel. Bicarb soda has a silky/powdery feel whereas washing soda is grainier and less silky.

The bicarb soda will need to reach the full 200° Celsius for this reaction to take place, so give it time.

Allow to cool and store in air-tight jar.

Super Grate Dishwash Liquid

Take a bar of soap, cut it into quarters, put aside one piece for this recipe and store the rest in a jar under the sink.

¼ BAR OF SOAP, GRATED

WATER

REPURPOSED SQUEEZY BOTTLE

1 TEASPOON ARROWROOT POWDER (OPTIONAL)

Tip grated soap into the bottle.

Pour in water, leaving a couple of centimetres clear at the top so you can shake the mixture thoroughly.

If you prefer a thicker dishwash liquid, add some arrowroot powder.

Shake before use and use sparingly: a little goes a long way!

Bulk Soap Extender

If you happen upon some liquid soap in bulk, this recipe will help you stretch it further. Store the large bottle of liquid soap in a large jar under the sink for when you need to top up.

---

3 TABLESPOONS WATER

1 TABLESPOON SEA SALT

1 TABLESPOON WASHING SODA (SEE PAGE 231)

1⅓ CUPS DISTILLED WATER

⅔ CUP BULK-BOUGHT LIQUID SOAP

2 TABLESPOONS FRESHLY SQUEEZED LEMON JUICE (OR THE ESSENTIAL OILS OF YOUR CHOICE)

REPURPOSED DISHWASH LIQUID DISPENSER

In a small saucepan, heat the water and salt, stirring until the salt is totally dissolved. Pour this into a bowl and set aside.

Add the washing soda and distilled water to the saucepan. Heat and stir until dissolved.

Carefully pour this into another bowl. Stir in the liquid soap and lemon juice or essential oils.

Add 1 spoon of the salt water to the soap and stir. It will turn cloudy and thicken. Add another tablespoon of the salt water mixture if you want it thicker. Keep in mind that it may thicken more over time.

Pour the mixture into a soap dispenser.

Citrus Dishwash Soap

The citrus in this soap offers antibacterial and antifungal properties plus helps cut through grease. While this soap definitely won't get the dishwater as sudsy as a store-bought product, that doesn't mean it won't shine up your china.

¼ CUP GRATED (OR BLENDED) NATURAL BAR SOAP

2 CUPS WATER

1–2 TABLESPOONS WHITE VINEGAR

1 TABLESPOON SOAPBERRY LIQUID (OPTIONAL; SEE PAGE 236)

1 TABLESPOON LEMON JUICE

1 TABLESPOON GRAPEFRUIT JUICE

3–5 DROPS ESSENTIAL OIL (OPTIONAL)

Pour the grated soap and water into a saucepan and place it on your stovetop over medium heat.

Stir the mixture until all the soap has melted into the water. Do not let it come to a boil. (Just turn down the heat if it seems like it's starting to simmer.)

Once the soap has all melted, remove the pan from heat. Allow the mixture to cool down for a few minutes.

Next, stir in the vinegar. Add soapberry liquid, if you've made some. This can help thicken the mix.

Allow the mixture to cool completely, then add the lemon and grapefruit juice. You can also add a few drops of your favourite essential oil at this stage, if desired. I used about 5 drops of lemon essential oil, for the fresh scent and extra cleaning power. Pour it into your preferred soap dispenser.

Sticky Residue Remover

Plastic labels often leave a sticky residue on glass. When you wish to store all of your gorgeous bulk foods in a display of zero-waste glory, sticky jars aren't really a part of that vision. Fortunately, it takes seconds to shine up your grimy jar. This Sticky Residue Remover is also good for tackling sludgy grime on surfaces and counter tops. Renae taught this to me on my Whale Shark Mermaid Retreat! Love my mermaids. So clever!

---

1 TEASPOON OLIVE OIL

1 TEASPOON BICARBONATE OF SODA (BAKING SODA)

Soak jar in warm water to loosen the glue.

Make a paste from the olive oil and bicarb.

Spread onto the sticky surface and allow it to sit for about 20 minutes.

With a sponge or scrubbing brush, scrub away the residue. Wash with warm water.

Soapberries: so good and so many uses

This is one of my all-time fave discoveries. The soapberry is the fruit of a tree that grows in abundance. When wet, they produce a soapy liquid that is 100% organic and natural and is super effective for all types of household cleaning. Plus it's antimicrobial, safe for septic systems, and gentle enough for use by sufferers of eczema, psoriasis and other skin conditions. At the end of their life, they're biodegradable, too, so you can pop them in your compost or garden.

The tree itself is the *Sapindus mukorossi,* and its round brown berries – which are about the size of a macadamia nut; in fact, some people call them soap nuts – are naturally high in saponin, Mother Nature's soap. They've been used for centuries in India, China, Nepal and neighbouring countries, and are rapidly becoming a staple in Western households. The trees take around nine years to mature and start producing the berries, but then they keep going for the next 80-plus years: gotta love a tree sucking carbon and cleaning the air. After the berries ripen and drop to the ground, they're collected and dried naturally in the sun. When the dried berries are mixed with water, you get soapy liquid. Who ever doubted that nature has it all!

In fact, the warmer the water, the more efficiently the saponin is released, so some people boil the soap berries in water to make a thick liquid. Or you can just soak a handful of soapberries in water for 24 hours, giving it a stir from time to time. Transfer the soapy liquid to a lidded jar. Repeat the process with the same berries; they keep releasing saponin for a while. To test, just squeeze the damp berry; a thick liquid should ooze out. When they've given their all, toss the spent berries in the compost. Beauty.

The liquid in your jar has a multitude of uses: as shampoo, hand-dishwashing liquid (maybe add some lemon essential oil), window wash or floor-cleaning detergent. You can also shampoo your pet with it. Remember not to expect thick white suds. Nature's way is clean, soft, comfortable, trustworthy! Not toxic and crisp or bleach white. Adjust your expectations and embrace the magic of this miraculous soaping berry!

To make a multipurpose spray, place ¼ to ½ cup of soapberry liquid in a recycled spray bottle, top up with water and add a few drops of essential oils, such as lavender, orange or eucalyptus. Soapberry liquid makes an effective pre-wash, too: scrub a few drops into soiled clothes or shirt collars – leave overnight for stubborn stains – then launder as normal in the washing machine.

Soapberries are primarily used for washing clothes, where their performance is every bit as good as most of those fancy chemical laundry detergents that are all too frequently packaged in plastic. Usually, soapberries are sold with one or two small drawstring cloth bags. For an average-sized wash, place 3–5 berries in one of the bags, secure it and toss it in the washing machine with your clothes. An old sock will do the same job. Hang the bag out to dry along with your washing as you can reuse the berries up to four times before the saponin runs down; then you compost the spent berries.

For a more intense wash, soak the bag of soapberries in a cup of boiling water and then toss it all (water included) in the washing machine. You can always boost the wash performance by adding a handful of baking soda or ¼ cup of white vinegar.

And as if there aren't enough benefits, the phosphate-free and chemical-free waste water from the wash is perfectly fine to use on your plants or to scrub your mossy concrete garden path.

Note that if soapberries absorb humidity, they will become sticky. They're still totally effective, but you might want to store them in a large airtight jar to keep them pleasant to handle.

Bathroom

The bathroom is second to the kitchen when it comes to generating waste — yet it's less obvious since our bathroom bin is mini compared to the kitchen bin. Notice what things you're throwing 'away'. Is there anything that can be replaced with a more sustainable option? Think cotton products packaged in cardboard, natural fibre floss in glass, even super-soft toilet tissue made from recycled paper.

Bathrooms are prone to scummy, icky build-up. Repurpose old sponges and brushes that are no longer suitable for the kitchen to deep-clean the toilet and bath.

Air Freshener

We are sensitive to smell. Keep this spray handy in the bathroom or anywhere else you think some good vibes are needed.

SMALL GLASS SPRAY BOTTLE

1 CINNAMON QUILL

FRESH LAVENDER BUDS

1 CUP WATER (OR LESS DEPENDING ON YOUR SPRAY BOTTLE CAPACITY)

2 TABLESPOONS VODKA OR REAL VANILLA EXTRACT

3 DROPS ESSENTIAL OILS

Slide the cinnamon quill down into the bottle and sprinkle in the lavender buds.

Pour in the water, then the vodka, then the essential oils.

Screw on the lid and give it a shake.

Write on a little cardboard sign 'Spray for Freshness'.

Toilet Polish

Okay, so no one is too worried about literally polishing the toilet. However, a shiny clean toilet is a trustworthy toilet, and who doesn't want to visit that every day? This recipe is easy and cheap and if any folks surprise visit — they'll be wowed at the all-natural sparkle in the loo.

---

2 TABLESPOONS
BICARBONATE OF
SODA

1 TABLESPOON
VINEGAR

2 DROPS OF
EUCALYPTUS
ESSENTIAL OIL

Pour bicarb soda into a small bowl.

Add vinegar and eucalyptus oil and stir with a spoon to form a paste.

Using scrunched up newspaper, dip in the paste and scrub the toilet till it shines!

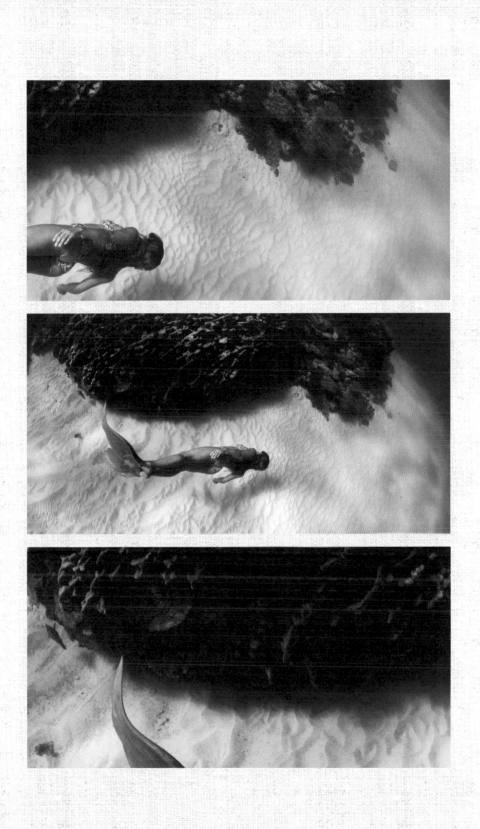

Laundry

MICROFIBRE POLLUTION

Currently, the dominant source of plastic in the ocean (rivalled by discarded fishing gear) is synthetic microfibres that detach from synthetic clothing when it's laundered. The agitation of the washing cycle shakes loose over 2000 fibres per wash, all of which gets pumped out through our pipes and into the waterways. Currently, water treatment plants don't filter out microscopic threads, so these flow on out to rivers and oceans.

The fashion industry is one of the top polluting industries in the world, and consumers continue to demand affordable fast fashion made from cheap synthetic fabric. This tells us that microfibres aren't going away. To cut down on the shedding of microfibres, our best option is to modify our approach to fashion and try to avoid buying, wearing and washing synthetic materials. But we express ourselves through fashion: it's important! When I wore natural colours for a year, blending into the landscape got me down. I rediscovered my pizazz in vintage clothes shops. Buying second hand is the go! Do note that second-hand synthetic materials may be old and worn and shed more fibres than new synthetic clothing, so wash by hand and dump the waste water in the backyard. It's far better for the garden to sift out the plastic fibres than the fish in our sea. Plus your clothes last longer with such special treatment!

I'm sure some imaginative innovators are out there solving this as I write, yet one problem with natural materials is that when they stretch out, they don't stretch back in. This makes swimwear and activewear a challenge. It feels like I spend half my time underwater and the other half on land bending in yoga positions, so I wear a lot of stretchy stuff.

My solution is to go for stretch material made from recycled plastic, such as retrieved fishing nets and carpets. Hopefully some epic natural stretchy material is on its way to our shelves soon. Until that happens, to minimise my contribution of microfibres, I'm careful with how I wash my stretchy swimwear, stretchy yogi clothes and stretchy undies.

THE BEST WAY TO WASH SYNTHETICS

I handwash synthetics in a separate tub or giant pot. Generally, I soak them for 10 minutes in cold water. If the activewear is smelly, I may add a teaspoon of vinegar to the soak. Then I add a small amount of soap (1 teaspoon usually works) and give them a bit of a wiggle. I give the spots where I sweat extra love — simply scrubbing the fabric against itself. Once I'm satisfied the items are clean, I pour the water into the garden, keeping the clothes in the tub. Then I fill the tub with more water for the clothing's final rinse. Lastly, I wring out each item by hand, hang everything on the line, and pour the tub into the next garden bed.

If washing by hand in a tub doesn't work for you, get a filter for your washing machine or redirect the grey water from your washing machine into the garden or lawn. Another option is a fibre-trapping washing bag; however, these are mostly synthetic, so also shed synthetic fibres.

WHERE CAN I START?

✳ Support slow fashion: buy local, hand-made, natural clothing from verified transparent sources.

✳ Challenge yourself to only buy second-hand or vintage clothes.

✳ Choose natural fibres over synthetic.

✳ Handwash garments made of synthetic fabric and pour the water on your plants.

✳ Wash less. Jeans in particular rarely need washing! They keep longer the less you wash them. If you want that tight fit, hang them in the shower to heat up with the humidity and then hang them out to dry in the heat of the day.

✳ Re-wear as much as possible. Spot-clean when you can.

✳ Try soapberries instead of detergent. Place the equivalent of 3–5 whole shells in the small wash bag provided, and throw in the wash with your clothes!

✳ Wash with cold water and use ⅓ of the soap you think you need.

✳ Go easy on water. Use the bare minimum and try to reuse it! If you boil the kettle and don't use all the water, pop the leftover in a thermos for later or take the opportunity to wash the floors or clean the countertops or flush the pipes!

✳ Line-dry your clothes: hang up a line and get yourself some wooden or stainless steel clothes pegs (clothes pins)! Sunshine is truly the best bleach you could ask for, plus the UV rays kill any microscopic fauna lurking in fabrics, and nothing beats the fresh air through your clothes.

✳ When you do use a dryer, ditch the synthetic dryer sheets and compost your lint.

✳ Using 100% wool dryer balls when you pop clothes in the dryer will ensure the garments come out soft. Look for balls packed in compostable paper not plastic.

✳ If you need to dry-clean garments, find an eco-friendly company that returns your clothes either in a reusable bag or no bag at all.

Powder Laundry Detergent

Natural laundry soap won't work as effectively as the laundry detergents full of chemicals scientifically designed to remove stains and brighten colours. However, our skin has to come in contact with our clothes after being washed in the harsh chemicals. This is a choice you have to make. I opt for healthy clothing. My body is quite sensitive to chemicals now, so when I wear clothes laundered in synthetic soaps I get itchy and my nose will run. Tune into the bod. She knows and will tell you what's up.

---

1 BAR SOAP (NATURAL, UNSCENTED; SEE PAGE 234)

Grate the bar soap or mix it in a blender until finely ground.

1 CUP WASHING SODA (BUY IN A CARDBOARD BOX OR SEE PAGE 231)

Place in a large glass jar. Add the remaining ingredients and shake.

1 CUP BORAX POWDER (BUY IN CARDBOARD BOX)

Use approximately 2 tablespoons or ¼ cup per wash.

½ CUP BICARBONATE OF SODA (BAKING SODA)

Soapberry Concentrated Liquid Laundry Detergent

Add about a tablespoon of this concentrate to each wash. For extra-soiled clothing, sprinkle in a tablespoon of bicarb soda.

---

20 SOAPBERRIES

2 LITRES WATER

Add the berries and water to a large saucepan and boil for 15–20 minutes.

Use the back of a large spoon to gently press the soft berries to squeeze out extra saponins. Be sure not to break them.

Allow to cool. Strain the liquid through your plant milk bag then pour into a large bottle.

To use, only a small amount is needed – a teaspoon to a tablespoon, depending on the wash size.

As this is a concentrate, store in the fridge to increase its lifespan.

Natural stain removal

I'm a big believer in the spot clean. If you spill something on your garment, get water into it straightaway. If you're effective, you won't have to wash the entire outfit. Good for you and for the planet.

Before you put your garments in the washing machine, moisten small stains and rub them with a stain stick made by wrapping a plain all-purpose bar soap in paper, to help get a grip. For stains that are harder to shift, spray with Soapberry Liquid (see page 236). For extra-tough stains, use Soapberry Concentrated Liquid Laundry Detergent (see page 246) and add some drops of eucalyptus essential oil. Apply directly to the stain, rub gently until the stain is released from the fabric, then add to your wash as per usual or rinse the spot clean and hang the garment to dry.

If you prefer to stockpile stained garments and then do a stain-removal blitz, reframe your attitude around this task: let this process be beautiful instead of a chore. Put some music on, light some incense and whip up your soapberry detergent.

As you pull out your basket of stained clothing, reflect on the story attached to each stain: how it got there and who you were with. The nature-connected life invites us to bring more presence and appreciation to tasks that wouldn't usually inspire awareness and reflection. But if we practise it, we enjoy all moments of life. We find ourselves laughing about the grass stains and the wine stains. Let all of life be a joy.

TO KEEP WHITES WHITE
Over time, whites tend to discolour. Always wash whites separately (save enough for a full load in your washer). These tips are designed to help whites retain their pristine glory. Bicarbonate of soda (baking soda), vinegar, borax, lemon juice and hydrogen peroxide all naturally whiten. Add ½ cup of any of these cleaners to each wash cycle to keep your clothes white. For double duty, mix in ½ cup vinegar and ½ cup borax to your white loads.

Borax and hydrogen peroxide don't always come packaged plastic free. If you can't find these products suitably packaged, stick with doubling the faithful lemon and bicarb!

The following tips are specific to certain colours or stains. For general stains, dab (don't rub) the area with lemon juice, vinegar or hydrogen peroxide, then launder as usual.

GRASS AND INK STAIN REMOVER
Drench the stain in cheap vodka and launder as usual.

RED WINE STAIN REMOVER
Immediately pour salt on the stain to absorb the moisture. Let the salt work its magic then gently shake it off. Next blot the stain with liberal amounts of club soda or sparkling water.

RUST STAIN REMOVER
Saturate the stain in lemon juice then sprinkle salt directly on it. Let the mixture react overnight then rinse it with cool water. Do not use hot water, as it will set the stain. Repeat these steps if the stain persists.

UNDERARM STAIN REMOVER
Remove yellow armpit stains by scrubbing the spots with bicarb soda and water. Mix together 4 tablespoons of bicarb soda and just enough water to form a paste. Scrub the mixture into the stains. Allow it to sit for a few minutes, then launder as usual. If the underarm areas of your garments tend to stain, treat that area before each washing – even if you can't see staining yet. If this is common for you, you may want to reduce your intake of spicy foods or slow down to ease the aggravation that's causing the staining sweat. For specific recommendations, you could book in for an Ayurvedic consultation.

White Soak

Regularly treat your whites to some TLC to prevent them from becoming dingy — or to resuscitate garments that have lost their brightness. Good laundering practices are the sensible alternative to fast fashion, and all the environmental vandalism it entails.

½ CUP WASHING SODA (SEE PAGE 231)

3.75 LITRES (1 GALLON) WATER

Stir washing soda into the water until dissolved.

Add soiled whites and leave to soak for 20–30 minutes.

Launder clothes as usual.

Note: The best bleach shines in the sky! Hang clothes to dry in the sun. This is the least expensive, all-natural whitener out there. The sun will naturally bleach the garments without setting stains like a dryer.

———

Lemon Soak

For clothes that haven't been white for quite a while, try this easy, natural method.

SAUCEPAN OF WATER

½ LEMON, SLICED

Fill a saucepan with water and add lemon slices.

Bring the water to a boil.

Turn off the heat and allow the mixture to cool until it's no longer steaming.

Fill a tub with the mixture and soak your sturdy fabrics, such as white linens, socks and non-delicate items until the water turns cold. Then add delicates. (Boiling hot water is hard on fabrics, especially delicates.)

Wash the clothes as usual and hang in the sun to dry.

Note: Lemon juice and hydrogen peroxide are high on the list of effective natural bleaches. Combining the two amps up the bleaching power.

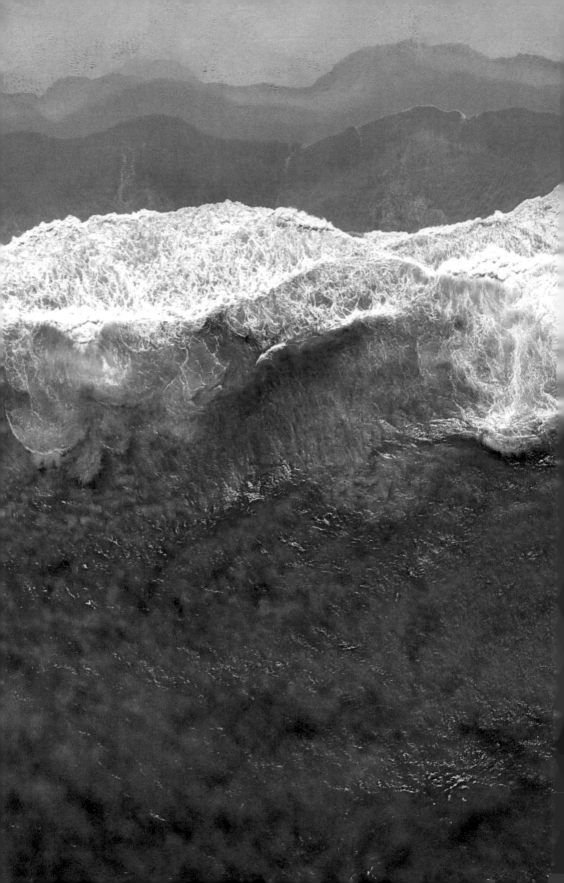

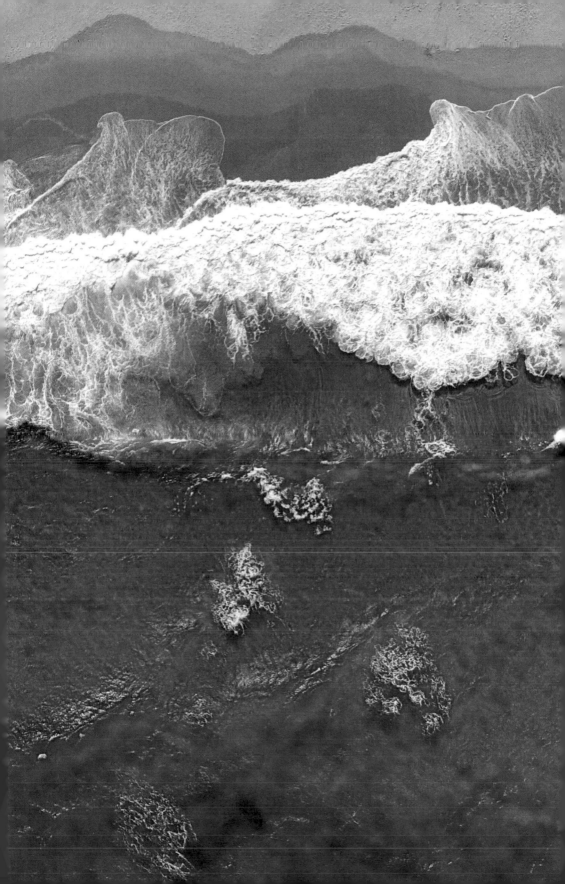

In closing

A RECIPE FOR INTUITION

I hope I have planted many seeds in your mind through the pages of this book. It is up to you to nurture these and support them to grow. Bring even a few of them into your routine and reap the benefits. Feel more vibrant in your body or enjoy the adventure back to nature.

In the closing of this text, I offer you a final recipe to make this process less cerebral. If you have ever struggled with what path to take, or making an important decision, or knowing how you truly feel or what you really need, this last recipe is for cultivating a relationship with your intuition. This is a recipe to follow in order to honour and connect with your higher self, the very part of your self that was called to this book and this way of life.

If we can quiet the mind, still the body, be present and listen, we hear more of the guidance to live the life we dream of for ourselves. This meditative ritual is to be practised and developed with your own style, to connect more with your higher consciousness, to lead a life of greater purpose, connection and awareness.

As with all of the recipes that I share with you, remember this is a basic beginning step to inspire you to try over and over until your own way unfolds. Then commit to this practice and honour the gifts and wisdom that are shared with you by returning often to this ritual.

WHY DO THIS?

As our life-force energy connects us with all beings, we are all one. We are all made up of cells, bacteria, energy. We have everything we ever need already inside of us. No one beyond our own selves can make us whole. No thing outside of us will ever make us complete. No clothes, no food, no soul mate. We are each already whole. We are perfect and complete just as we are.

The sooner we feel this deeply with unwavering trust and security, the sooner we stop grasping outward for validation and fulfilment. The sooner we are content by being inwardly connected. The sooner we heal. The sooner the world heals.

What more can we want? The path is inward.

Let the Earth hold you, as she always has and always will.

Let your self find the way back.

Namaste – Ashei – Aho – Amen

Higher self meditation

Stand firmly.

Close your eyes.

Feel the Earth beneath you, supporting and holding you to the planet.

Remember you are nature.

Breathe deeply.

Let every breath be longer, slower, deeper than the one before.

Feel the oxygen filling your lungs, infusing your blood, which will travel your body nourishing your tissues.

Bring one hand to your belly.

This energy centre is what drives you forward in life: honour the power here in your core.

Bring one hand to your heart.

Present to all the love within you, and thinking of something or many things that you are grateful for.

Let this gratitude wash over you, and come back to the glowing space of your heart.

Feel into yourself. Intentionally seeking your higher self.

What is it you need?

What is it you desire?

Can you hear your intuition?

Can you hear guidance?

Often it is the first words we hear.

Or simply a knowing.

Not the shouting of the ego.

Or the doubt that slinks in, telling you this is a waste of time.

If you need specific guidance, ask a question.

Listen for the answer.

Feel for the answer.

Take a few slow, deep breaths.

Return to the feeling of gratitude.

Grateful for this small pause you have gifted yourself.

Grateful for this quiet time you have allowed for deeper connection to your spirit.

Welcoming this voice of intuition to guide you.

Welcoming the courage to follow.

Open your eyes.

Take a deep breath and sigh.

Thank yous

I owe many a thank you to so many amazing humans for housing me as I wrote and experimented in their kitchens with plants and blenders and flowers and jars. Most were rewarded for this with entertainment and treats. Here is an extra serving of gratitude for this gift of supporting me in the journey to finish this book and on my non-conformist crusade to rid the world of plastics. It was not always an easy path. I am incredibly grateful for your love and support and for backing me. I will never forget this.

I shall pass my individual thanks on in person to my friends and family mentors and the mermaids who supported me.

I put my thanks in print to my dear, sweet father. Who has supported me in all ways without question. As I walked a path unlike any other and committed to the environment when most others committed to corporate and marriage. He offered his shoulder and had my back. His unconditional love has lifted me through many dark times. Without him, I may have wavered on this path. Thank you, Dad. I love you.

Recommended reading

Michael Pollan, *Food Rules: An Eater's Manual*, Penguin Books, London, 2010.

Christopher Hedley and Non Shaw, *Herbal Remedies: A Practical Beginner's Guide to Making Effective Remedies in the Kitchen*, Parragon, Bath, UK, 1999.

Joanna Macy and Chris Johnstone, *Active Hope: How to face the mess we're in without going crazy*, New World Library, Novato, USA, 2011.
See also joannamacy.net

Rachel Carson, *Silent Spring*, First Mariner Books, New York, 2002.

Charles Massy, *Call of the Reed Warbler: A New Agriculture — A New Earth*, University of Queensland Press, St Lucia, 2017.

Don Miguel Ruiz, *Four Agreements: A Practical Guide to Personal Freedom*, Amber-Allen Publishing, San Rafael, USA, 1997.

Yvon Chouinard and Vincent Stanley, *The Responsible Company: What we've learned from Patagonia's first 40 years*, Ventura, USA, 2012.

Leonardo Trasande, *Fatter, Sicker, Poorer: The urgent threat of hormone-disrupting chemicals to our health and future ... and what we can do about it*, Houghton Mifflin Harcourt Publishing Company, New York, 2019.

Anthony G. Jay, *Estrogeneration: How Estrogenics Are Making You Fat, Sick, and Infertile*, Pyrimidine Publishing, Tallahassee, USA, 2017.

For more philosophy, recipes, science and interviews with experts:
Kate Nelson vlog: youtube.com/c/plasticfreemermaid
iquitplastics.com

Photo credits

The author and publisher are grateful to the following photographers for permission to use their artwork:

Shifaaz Shamoon, cover photograph and endpapers

Ryo Yoshitake, page 13

Lu Castoldi, pages vi, 63, 67, 75, 104, 129 167, 173, 191, 219, 258, 264

Norm Nelson, pages viii, 263

Nico Filgueira, pages 8, 185, 201

Erin Ireland, pages 20, 58, 71, 72, 89, 111, 112, 123, 126, 131, 152, 207, 225

Alex Kydd, pages 27, 149, 155, 161, 189, 241

Andrzej Kryszpiniuk, page 38

Tetiana Bykovets, page 77

Luigi Pozzoli, page 84

Eiliv-Sonas Aceron, pages 119-120

Ines Álvarez Fdez, pages 138 139

Gatis Marcinkevics, page 177

Mourad Saadi, page 211

Joel Vodell, pages 252-253

All other photographs are from the private collection of Kate Nelson.

About the author

WHO IS THIS MERMAID?

Raised with environmental values and hours of family service work, Kate Nelson spent much of her free time volunteering for ocean conservation organisations. To preserve the oceans, Kate gave up disposable plastics over ten years ago and has been campaigning against plastic pollution ever since. Kate has now phased out plastics from all areas of her life and has taught herself to make everything at home from natural ingredients.

With the forests, rivers, beaches and oceans rapidly filling up with our plastic waste, Kate has made it her mission to share these recipes, to refocus people on the magic of nature, and to remind people to respect our Earth.

iquitplastics.com

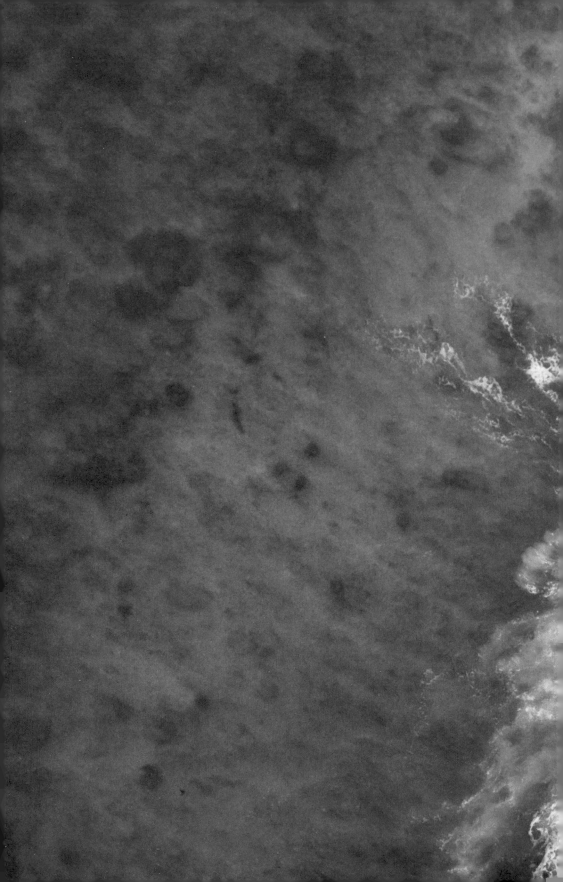